## PRAISE FOR *Never Shoot a Stampede Queen*

Mark Leiren-Young is the funniest writer you've never heard from. *Never Shoot a Stampede Queen* is a terrific debut: funny, moving and profound. You will laugh out loud.

—**Will Ferguson, author**

Mark Leiren-Young has earned an enviable reputation as a Canadian comic and storyteller, but here he expands his literary horizon. His portrait of small-town BC is a mixture of Leacock (the wry humour and evocative literary style) and Freud (psychoanalyzing the rural psyches of his cast of kooky characters). It's a must-read, and fun too.

—**Peter C. Newman, author**

*Never Shoot a Stampede Queen* isn't just sound advice, it's also the most fun I've had this year. God does not subtract from one's allotted span the hours spent reading books as wise, warm and witty as this City Mouse's comic memoir of his years in the Country . . . of another planet. Indeed, the residents of remote Williams Lake, in the heart of the Cariboo, satisfy science fiction editor John W. Campbell's classic definition of alien creatures: they think as well as a human being, but not *like* one. Mark Leiren-Young is a natural storyteller, a peer of writers like Stephen Leacock, W. O. Mitchell, Jack Douglas and W. P. Kinsella: quietly hilarious, effortlessly moving, and always surprising. Like them, he makes it look easy.

—**Spider Robinson,**
**co-author (with Robert A. Heinlein) of *Variable Star***

We have known for a long, long time that Mark is a wonderful writer, mostly because he keeps telling us, and this book only confirms it. If you are a young journalist you should read this book. If you're an old journalist, you should read it. If you're a young rodeo queen, or an old rodeo queen or any member of any kind of royalty at all, you should read it. Heck, if you can read and you are mostly alive, you should read this book. We did, and we are better for it.

—**Bob Robertson and Linda Cullen,**
**a.k.a. comedy duo Double Exposure**

Mark Leiren-Young is the funniest guy I know, and I know a lot of inadvertently funny people. The difference is that Mark is advertently funny. Watching him perform, I think I'm too old to giggle, but giggle I do. I feel I'm too distinguished to guffaw at his antics, but I guffaw at them anyway. I know my hearing is not as good as it once was, but when I listen to him it is better than it ever was. And when I read what he writes—for instance, these stories, skits, routines, recollections, reminiscences, whatnots, etc.—I know that my eyesight is as sharp as ever. Mark is advertently funny and what a relief that is! The first sentence of each tale grabs my attention and holds on tight. Ninety or so lines later—three or four pages (I have counted them!—he leaves me smiling and anxious to begin yet another of his improbable tales about the life of "a reporter in the boonies." The Cariboo has never looked so . . . dangerous! If *Never Shoot a Stampede Queen* is not shortlisted for the Leacock Medal for Humour, the ashes of old Stephen should turn over in his urn at St. George's Anglican Church, Sibbald Point, Ontario.

—**John Robert Colombo, author and anthologist**

Loved it! I'm going to make sure my old journalism pals read it— it has universal themes/struggles of hilarity/triumphs/awesome defeats common to our practice and was downright poignant at times. This reminded me how small towns are unique in their level of eccentricity. I salute you, sir.

—**Zachary Petit, Managing Editor, *Writer's Digest***

Always engaging and often hilarious . . . *Stampede Queen* is an absolute charmer in the Stuart McLean/Will Ferguson vein.

—**John Threlfall, *Monday Magazine***

Williams Lake comes across as the Wild West mixed with Capone-era Chicago with a soupçon of Jim Crow Deep South segregation and an unsavory dash of perversion. And that's just in the first chapter.

—**Tom Hawthorn, *The Globe and Mail***

For a cub reporter from Vancouver, working deep in British Columbia's cowboy country was like a mission to Mars . . . In his first book, *Never Shoot a Stampede Queen: A Rookie Reporter in the Cariboo*, a young Leiren-Young recounts wild times in one of B.C.'s wildest towns, Williams Lake. The result is a hilarious ride through a western town, complete with gun fights, bar fights, plane crashes and, of course, mad bombers, all as seen through the fresh eyes of a newbie reporter for the *Williams Lake Tribune*.

—**Randy Shore,** *Vancouver Sun*

For the record, I worked at the Williams Lake Tribune after Mark Leiren-Young did. I'm not the wacko editor or overly-protective senior reporter he talks about in his new book *Never Shoot a Stampede Queen: A Rookie Reporter in the Cariboo*. (I was the wacko editor who worked there after Leiren-Young left.) However, I do know all the people Leiren-Young talks about in his book. That's probably why I liked his book so much. I could put faces to the bevy of characters he describes. So, take it from me, he does describe them very well. If you want an accurate description of how life was (or is) like at a small-town newspaper, read his book. It is laced with humour, truth, and unbelievable people . . . I can vouch for the fact that he did not make up the characters in his book. They are real and they're worth reading about. You'll shake your head, your jaw will drop, and you'll laugh.

—**Bill Phillips,** *Prince George Free Press*

The book itself is city-boy-meets-really-rural-life and the hilarity that ensues. But it's more than that, due to Leiren-Young's wry commentary, amusing observations and, most importantly, his success at not dismissing the Cariboo folk as yokels existing for his amusement. True, the fish-out-of-water plot drives this tale, and the characters Leiren-Young encounters are certainly memorable, but he does not mock them. On more than a few occasions, the author notes in subtle ways how his city-slicker ways might not be as progressive as he once believed . . . *Never Shoot a Stampede Queen* is 221 pages of rip-roarin' Cariboo craziness that you simply won't be able to put down.

—**Christopher Foulds,** *Kamloops This Week*

*Never Shoot a Stampede Queen* could serve as the one-book answer to everything would-be journos ever ask—or need to know—about what it's like to be a real reporter. (Short answer: hilarious when it's not astounding, frustrating, or terrifying.) Not that Mark Leiren-Young, a journalist turned comedian, playwright, TV-scriptwriter, and author, intended the "memoir" of his first reporting gig in a community daily to turn into a textbook. It's much too funny a page-turner to be ignored on required-reading lists.

—Shannon Rupp, *J-Source*

There is a universal appeal for a well told tale, and Leiren-Young's tales are well told indeed. He's a funny, sharp writer who doesn't slip into toilet humour to make a joke. At the same time, he shows a great sensitivity regarding topics that aren't funny, like murders in a small town or racism.

—Allison Vail, *Ladysmith Chronicle*

I received your book, *Never Shoot a Stampede Queen*, a week ago for my birthday. I am from Williams Lake, BC, and have lived here for the majority of my life. I am also the 2008/2009 Williams Lake Stampede Queen. I absolutely LOVE your book. Everytime I read it I burst out laughing. The part with the photos of the queen contestants and how important they are to the girls was so accurate. When I got my pictures done everything had to be just perfect. When people asked me why I wanted to run for Williams Lake Stampede Queen I can't count the number of times I responded with a predictable "I've always wanted to be a Stampede Queen." I just want to say that I think your book is great and it was a perfect birthday present :)

—Britnie McKnight, 2008–2009 Williams Lake Stampede Queen

# NEVER
# SHOOT A
# STAMPEDE
# QUEEN

## A ROOKIE REPORTER IN THE CARIBOO

Mark Leiren-Young

Victoria · Vancouver · Calgary

Heritage House Publishing Company Ltd.
#108–17665 66A Avenue
Surrey, BC  V3S 2A7
www.heritagehouse.ca

Heritage House Publishing Company Ltd.
PO Box 468
Custer, WA
98240-0468

Library and Archives Canada Cataloguing in Publication.

Leiren-Young, Mark
    Never shoot a Stampede Queen: a rookie reporter in the Cariboo / Mark Leiren-Young.

ISBN 978-1-894974-52-3

    1. Leiren-Young, Mark. 2. Tribune (Williams Lake, B.C.: 1967).
3. Williams Lake (B.C.)—Anecdotes. 4. Canadian wit and humor (English).
5. Reporters and reporting—British Columbia—Williams Lake—Biography.
6. Williams Lake (B.C.)—Biography. I. Title.

PN4913.L44A3 2008          070.4'3092          C2008-905393-1

Library of Congress Control Number: 2008930359


Edited by Karla Decker
Proofread by Marial Shea
Cover and book design by Clint Hutzulak/Mutasis Creative
Cover photo by Matt Knowles

Printed in Canada

Mixed Sources
Cert no. SW-COC-001271
© 1996 FSC
FSC

The interior of this book was printed on 100% post-consumer recycled paper, processed chlorine free and printed with vegetable-based inks.

Heritage House acknowledges the financial support for its publishing program from the Government of Canada through the Book Publishing Industry Development Program (BPIDP), Canada Council for the Arts and the province of British Columbia through the British Columbia Arts Council and the Book Publishing Tax Credit.

Canada Council
for the Arts

Conseil des Arts
du Canada

BRITISH
COLUMBIA
ARTS COUNCIL
Supported by the Province of British Columbia

In 1988, I wrote these stories for
Darron Eibbitt-McFadyen (now Leiren-Young),
so she'd know who I was when I went to Williams Lake.

In 2008, I rewrote them for Jenny McPhee,
so she'd know who her mother was back before
Wendy was a mom and she was my hero.

# Contents

# *Foreword*

Y̶ou are in for a treat. Like discovering a new flavour of ice cream you've never tried before is a treat. And you love it. And it is instantly your new favourite flavour. Right? Or you hear a song from an unknown singer or a band you've never listened to before and—wham—where has that music been all your life?

Or, like now, you pick up a brand-new book from a first-time author and right from the very first page, from the very first paragraph, from the very first sentence, you are thinking "I am not going to be able to put this down."

That's what they call a "quick read," by the way—whoever "they" are. It just means that once you start reading, you don't stop until you are finished. Because it is that good.

Like this book.

*Never Shoot a Stampede Queen* is lightning-fast and fiercely funny, and if you've got an early morning planned tomorrow, you should skip the rest of this foreword and start reading right now, because you are going to miss out on some sleep.

Mark Leiren-Young may be a first-time author, but he sure ain't no first-time writer. He's the Real Deal and He Does This For A Living. I laughed out loud on every page, and I've heard most of these stories before.

Full disclosure time. Mark and I have been friends, really good friends, for some 20 years and counting. We've had curiously parallel careers, but I've never written a play with the depth of his *Shylock* or with the humanity of his *Blueprints From Space*. He was one-half of one of the best comedy duos this country ever produced, and if you are already a Local Anxiety fan, you don't need me to tell you how funny he is. Oh, yeah, he just wrote and directed a feature film—a full-length movie called *The Green Chain*—and it is timely and well directed and brilliantly written.

It is a sign of our mutual respect that we haven't let the fact that he's a better writer than me get in the way of our friendship.

All of which is to tell you that you've made an excellent choice. You are in on the ground floor, and years and years down the road you'll be able to take credit for buying the first-ever book written by Mark Leiren-Young. Before everybody else jumps on the bandwagon and the bestseller lists and awards start rolling in. The thrill of discovery, right? Like that ice cream. Speaking of discovery, don't the folks at Heritage House look sharp, eh? Means they were just smart enough to snap up this astonishingly good book from this amazingly talented writer. It's a terrific read, full of funny bits and some scary bits and even some sad bits. Enjoy. And welcome to the Mark Leiren-Young fan club. I'm one of the charter members.

Ian Ferguson
Vancouver, British Columbia
July 2008

*Ian Ferguson won the Stephen Leacock Memorial Medal for Humour in 2004 for his memoir* Village of the Small Houses. *With his brother, Will Ferguson, he is the co-author of* How To Be A Canadian, *which was shortlisted for the Leacock in 2002 and also won the Libris Award for best non-fiction book the same year.*

# *Introduction*

The cops wanted to shoot me, my bosses thought I was a Bolshevik, and a local lawyer warned me that some people I was writing about might try to test the strength of my skull with a steel pipe. What more could any young reporter hope for from his first real job?

Most people know the Cariboo—if they know it at all—courtesy of Paul St. Pierre, who immortalized the stoic cowboys and ranch-hand philosophers in his collections of true stories and truish tall tales. St. Pierre created a whole mythology out of the type of characters Gabby Hayes played in westerns—quirky cowboy charmers and people who don't get meaner when they drink, just quirkier. When I went to the Cariboo I'd never heard of the place—but I had met St. Pierre.

I was a 15-year-old high school student, and he was introduced to me as a famous writer. I'd never heard of him, but I was a Canadian kid growing up in the '70s, so I'd never heard of any Canadian writers besides Margaret Atwood and Farley Mowat. And I'd only heard of them because I had a hippie English teacher who believed Canadians could write. I was also lucky enough to have another teacher who made sure I ended up in St. Pierre's workshop for a dozen "promising" young writers from Vancouver. I only remember one piece of advice from St. Pierre: "Don't talk about something or you'll never write it."

It was great advice, but in my case, I never would have written this if I hadn't shared the stories with friends who told me I'd be crazy if I didn't write a book. So two years after I left Williams

Lake, in the fall of 1986, when I was so sick with mono that I couldn't stand long enough to leave my apartment, I wrote a collection of 35 stories. And when I was finally able to go outside, I had the stories copied and bound at Kinko's and sent them out as Christmas and Chanukah gifts to family and friends. I took a brief shot at publishing them before setting the book aside for reasons that made sense at the time. A few years ago my friend Kennedy Goodkey asked if he could perform some of the stories on stage—in Australia. After seeing audiences get caught up in these stories thousands of miles away from BC, he asked why I'd never published them. More recently, two other friends—Art Norris and Ian Ferguson, whose wonderful debut novels you really have to read—asked the same question.

Since I couldn't come up with an answer, I took another look at the stories, revised them with the help of Ian's editor, Barbara Pulling, and sent them back out into the world. I tried to avoid making too many changes in order to be as faithful as possible to the 22-year-old aspiring journalist who lived them. So the stories are as true as my memory can make them. The names and a few details have been changed—and some real people are now what the lawyers like to call "composite characters" —in the hopes that my friends in the Cariboo will still talk to me after they read this, and to avoid giving my publisher's lawyer a heart attack.

For what it's worth, I find a lot of these stories hard to believe too. I found them even harder to believe when they were happening.

# Bomb Blasts Cariboo Courtroom

The question I get asked most about that afternoon is why I stayed. If the bomb strapped to the defendant's chest went off, I could die. If the undercover cop sitting next to me pulled his gun, I could die. Depending on how powerful the bomb was, everyone in the courtroom could die. And the would-be bomber was less than 10 feet away from me.

There were only eight people in court that morning. And I was the only one who could leave without disrupting the trial. If the cowboy judge, the pumpkin-shaped sheriffs, the ambitious young prosecutor or the twitchy stenographer moved, the bomber might panic.

The undercover cop wasn't going anywhere.

And Roland Kyle Fraser definitely couldn't leave the room, because he was on trial for sexually assaulting his children and attempting to murder his ex-wife. But I was just a rookie reporter for the local newspaper—and I was only a few feet from the door, so I was pretty sure I could make it to the exit before anyone started shooting. Or exploding.

I wasn't even supposed to be there. I hadn't come to the courthouse to cover Fraser's trial. I was there for "real" news. The Williams Lake Timberwolves had been in a brawl a few weeks earlier with the Grande Prairie Chiefs. A hockey fight isn't news in Canada—although a game without one might be, especially in a rugged logging town like Williams Lake. But this time it wasn't a player who scored the knockout punch. One of the hometown fans got a little over-enthusiastic, hopped the boards and nailed one of Grande Prairie's forwards, breaking his nose. Since the ref couldn't give the fan a penalty, the police jumped over the boards, slipped, skidded and slid after the soon-to-be "accused," tackled him and charged him with assault.

Not only was this a natural page-one story for my paper, the venerable *Williams Lake Tribune*, but it was the type of crazy Cariboo tale I knew I'd be able to resell to one of the big dailies in Vancouver. And the more stories I sold to the papers back home, the faster I'd be getting out of the Cariboo.

Just before I walked into the courtroom I'd bumped into the public defender, Lyle Norton. The bald, bored 40ish lawyer flashed a weird little grin before declaring, "It's gonna be an interesting one." I knew the case was going to be interesting, and assumed he was gloating.

Lyle had already tipped me to his strategy, which is why I'd blocked two days off to cover the trial. His defence was that if the players could hit each other, there was nothing wrong with a little audience participation. The Vancouver editors would love that. If Lyle was quotable enough, I figured I might even be able to sell the story to a paper in Toronto or maybe—if Lyle was really quotable—*Maclean's* magazine. The national media loves stories about wacky westerners.

"The hockey trial should be fun," I said.

"The hockey trial's been postponed," said Lyle. Then, before there was time to drop a puck, he deked into one of the four-storey building's two elevators and disappeared.

I glanced at the schedule pinned next to the courtroom door. Checking that list was part of my daily ritual. I hadn't memorized all the criminal code numbers yet—just the ones that added up to news, like violent crimes and "Theft over . . . " And when I saw a series of 150s that translated to a variety of sexual assaults, an attempted murder, and incest, I knew there was no story. Even if the idea of covering an incest trial wasn't sickening, the publication ban to protect the victim's identity meant I'd have a tough time writing much more than "some nameless creep was charged with doing something vile."

I was just turning to chase Lyle upstairs to get the new dates for the hockey trial when the Crown counsel, Kevin Holland, spotted me at the door and told me I really ought to leave. "You don't want to bother with this one," he said. "It'll be boring."

So I opened the courtroom door, and Holland trailed me inside. I was raised on American cop shows, so one of the first lessons I learned covering trials was that "Crown counsel" is Canadian for "prosecutor." Holland was a slick legal prodigy in his mid-20s who'd come to Williams Lake to rack up trial time before moving back to the big city, where he seemed destined to run for political office after making his first million as a corporate lawyer. "It's just a run-of-the-mill sexual assault trial," said Holland.

Run of the mill? Was that why Holland looked ready to tackle me as I approached the little wooden bench, just inside the door, known as the press box? He was still telling me how boring the trial was going to be as I took off my leather aviator jacket, flipped open my purple University of Victoria clipboard and shuffled into my seat.

Then Constable Ron Crofton came through the door. Crofton was a cheerful officer in his early 30s who looked like he'd just stepped out of an RCMP recruiting poster. He even sported the official moustache the RCMP used to issue along with the badges. But instead of a uniform, Constable Ron was dressed in civvies. And instead of heading to the public gallery—the half-dozen rows at the back where the police were supposed to sit with the citizens—he scrunched in next to me. In the six months I'd covered trials in Williams Lake, the press box had always been reserved for press. It was set up so reporters could see the entire courtroom—the judge's bench to the left, the public gallery to the right, the defence table and witness box a few feet in front and the Crown counsel's desk beyond that. The press had a slightly better view than the police, but this wasn't a big courtroom.

"I'm a reporter," said Constable Ron, as a goofy grin spread across his face. He flashed an empty steno pad. "See, this is my notebook."

"Okay," I said in my best conspiratorial whisper. "If you're a reporter, I'm a policeman."

Constable Ron shushed me and his grin vanished. Then, seriously this time, as if he were issuing an order: "I'm a reporter."

"Okay, you're a reporter."

Constable Ron nodded. Curiouser and curiouser.

The press box was like an undersized penalty box, with a shelf that flipped up to act as a writing desk. And having something to write on was important, since the first lesson I'd learned covering trials was that recording devices were illegal and a misquote could land you in jail on contempt charges. The desk was now in the up position, so I definitely wasn't prepared when Holland strode over to visit my new "reporter" friend and flipped open the latch, causing the shelf to flop down, bounce against the box's inside wall, and barely miss smashing my knees. I didn't have time to ask anything before Holland explained, "Just in case Constable Crofton has to do what he's trained to do."

Run of the mill?

Holland retreated to his table. The sheriffs were in position at the back of the court. The stenographer was at her desk beside the judge's bench. And that was when the door opened again and the defendant walked in.

Williams Lake courtrooms were pretty casual. After all, with folks in these parts, clean jeans counted as formal wear. But this guy's hair was flying like it had barely survived a lightning storm. He was draped in a bulky camper's coat, with a huge backpack in tow. And I'm sure if I'd made the effort, I could have smelled him before he entered the room. The stenographer looked up at him, then went back to her stenography. The two sheriffs, who looked like Tweedledum and Tweedledee, barely glanced up. A moment later, when Judge Quentin Turner entered through his chamber door at the front of the courtroom, everyone stood like we were supposed to. But as soon as the judge was seated, we all looked around again because someone was definitely missing from this picture.

"Where's defence counsel?" asked Judge Turner.

That's when the accused rose and stood at the defence table to address the bench. "I have decided to act as my own attorney," said Fraser. "I have consulted with counsel, and Mr. Norton advised me to plead guilty. I am most definitely not going to do that."

Judge Turner was startled, but firm and judgelike. "I suggest perhaps you may want to meet with another lawyer, discuss your case and—"

Fraser interrupted. "No, your honour. I have decided to act as my own attorney." Judge Turner responded like a parent explaining the dangers of touching a stove. "That really isn't a very good idea."

Fraser continued to argue, sounding like someone who'd just finished studying all the big legal words and was itching to use them all in a sentence—ideally, the same sentence. Then the judge asked Fraser how he wanted to plead.

"I'm not going to enter a plea," said Fraser. "I'll do that later. After you've heard all the evidence. After everything has been heard."

Judge Turner repeated that a lawyer would be a fine idea, and a plea would be an even better one. Fraser kept repeating that he intended to represent himself. They kept at this for almost half an hour before Judge Turner reluctantly conceded that Fraser could act as his own attorney. Fraser looked like he'd already won the case. "I want all the facts to come out," he said to the judge. "All of the facts." Then he took a book from his faded backpack—Plato's *Republic*—and placed it gently on the defence table, like it was a family bible. This was either his legal text, or Mr. Fraser was dealing with some very old facts.

"The guy's nuts," I whispered to Constable Ron.

He shushed me.

After Fraser pulled out his book, I thought about how bizarre it was that someone on trial for attempted murder was allowed to carry a backpack into a courtroom. I was just thinking, *What if there's something dangerous in*—when he took off his coat.

Nobody actually gasped, but I think that's just because almost everyone had stopped breathing. Fraser was wearing a robin's-egg blue turtleneck sweater with the turtle-top pulled halfway up around his unshaven neck. And beneath the sweater, just over his heart was . . . something. Something big. Something that looked awfully like . . . I turned towards Constable Ron and scrawled a quick note in my steno pad. "What the hell is that?"

"I don't know," he wrote back. "What do you think it is?"

One of the sheriffs scowled at Constable Ron and me like he'd caught us chewing gum in class. Everyone else in the courtroom looked like they were trying to carry on with business as usual—despite having forgotten how to breathe. Everyone except Fraser and the judge.

"It's probably my overactive imagination," I scribbled, "but I think it's a bomb." Constable Ron nodded. I didn't want him to nod. I was hoping he'd laugh.

I filled the rest of the page with very large letters spelling out, "Am I losing my mind?" Constable Ron took my notepad, flipped the page over and scrawled, "I'll discuss it with you later." I nodded. Then he added, "If we both get out of here alive."

The only thing I knew for sure was that if I was going to die, I was going to die next to the only cop in Williams Lake with a sense of humour.

# Cookie Strikers
# Batter Boss

///

$B$efore we get to how I ended up in the court-room that morning, I should probably start with how I ended up in Williams Lake in the first place. How does anyone get from Vancouver to Williams Lake? By accident.

I was about to enter the job market with a freshly minted Bachelor of Fine Arts in Theatre and Creative Writing—recognized in better restaurants worldwide as a waiter's degree—when my friend Sheryl offered me a job as artistic director of a children's theatre company in Ontario. Children's theatre wasn't exactly my dream but . . . *Artistic Director*. I liked the sound of that. Sheryl even offered to drive with me to Ontario to help get things rolling.

My girlfriend Barb took the news well. She didn't break anything. And we came up with a plan. We both knew that all writers in Canada had to move to Toronto eventually—and we were both writers—so this job would give me an excuse to set up a place there. Once I'd settled in, she'd drive out and join me.

So I stuffed everything I could fit into the shiny new Toyota Celica I'd scored as a grad gift from my family, and Sheryl and I set off to the promised land. We spent three days talking about the theatre company and how I'd get the chance to write, direct, even act if I felt like it. Sheryl told me about touring around the small-town schools, how great the audiences were and how much fun she'd had doing the job for the last five summers. By the time we arrived she'd almost talked herself into staying to run the company again.

She set me up in her parents' basement and that's where I was—lying on the bed, reading one of the children's plays I was planning to stage—when she knocked on the open door and looked at me like someone had died. Her friend had forgotten to file the grant application in time. Her theatre company—my theatre company—was gone. I put down the script and stared at the wall. How was I supposed to stay in Ontario if I didn't have a job?

Sheryl couldn't stop apologizing. She was even more upset than I was. Her parents said they'd let me stay with them for free until I found something else to do. That night Sheryl decided to take me over to her brother Dwayne's for a visit, to cheer me up.

Dwayne and his wife, Brenda, served chewy oatmeal cookies and tea, and talked to Sheryl about life at university. I sat there thinking about the theatre company. Maybe there was still a way to save it. Maybe we could appeal to the granting agency or find private funding? I had to do something.

After Sheryl finished talking about the show she was going to direct in Vancouver—playing it down, so I wouldn't actually die of jealousy—she asked Dwayne about "the problems at the factory." Dwayne, a wiry 30-year-old, born-again Christian—started talking in a calm, born-again monotone about "the strike."

"It's getting pretty violent," he said. "There are guards around the factory to prevent sabotage and a few days ago, some of the guys on the line attacked me." He lifted a finger to his cheek and pointed to the fading remnants of a black eye.

"Sounds pretty ugly," I said, picturing a mob of angry Teamsters pummeling this small, sweet man to the ground.

"It is."

"What kind of factory?" I asked sympathetically.

"Cookies."

"Cookies," I squealed.

"Yeah, these kind," he said, pointing to the chewy little oatmeal rings we'd been munching.

"You were beaten up by cookie strikers?" My mind reeled. I'd always thought cookies were baked by happy little elves or something.

"Yes."

And that's when I lost it. I let loose with a maniacal laugh that just wouldn't stop. "I'm sorry," I said, gasping for air.

I knew I shouldn't laugh—that cookies were this man's livelihood, and he'd been hurt, and he was Sheryl's brother and I was a guest in his home and . . . Then I'd say "cookie strikers" again and keep howling as I pictured marauding gangs of cookie elves beating up on poor, born-again Dwayne.

When I finally returned to what passed for normal for me, I tried to apologize. "I didn't mean to laugh," I explained, "but I just can't picture," and then I giggled again, "cookie strikers." I began imagining possible forms of cookie sabotage—substituting butterscotch for chocolate chips or spiking vanilla extract with vodka. I felt another giggle fit coming on and bit my lip—hard—so I wouldn't start laughing again.

"That's okay," said Dwayne in a tone that seemed to absolve me. "Actually, I thought that maybe since you needed a job right now you might want to do some work for me until this whole thing with the theatre company gets sorted out." He smiled like he was making me an offer I couldn't refuse. "Six bucks an hour."

"That's very nice of you," I said, and just as I was about to start laughing again I realized that if I didn't find work soon I might actually have to become a scab at a cookie factory and risk being beaten and battered by little cookie elves. It's not like I had any better offers. And that knocked all the giggles right out of me.

It was the prospect of the cookie factory that convinced me to swallow my pride—and another oatmeal ring—and phone home to confess that I'd driven across the country for a few free cookies. I couldn't tell Barb, though. Not yet. We had a plan, and me driving back to BC wasn't it.

"Hi, Mom."

I explained that I had enough money to last about two months, and if I didn't find something by June I'd head home.

Mom sounded concerned, the way mothers are supposed to, but I told her not to worry. "Something will turn up," I suggested hopefully.

Three hours later, something did. My mother called back from her office. "Phone your brother."

I phoned home. David told me someone had called from Williams Lake to offer me a reporting job. He'd told the caller I was working in Ontario, but that I might need something at the end of the summer. He'd taken the number just in case. The timing was incredible enough, but the real miracle was that David took a phone message. David never took messages.

I dialed the number, and the voice at the other end was deep and jovial—a big man's voice. "That sure was quick," he said. "I thought you were working in Ontario."

"I am," I said, "but I might be interested in moving back to BC. I'm, uh, very homesick."

The guy introduced himself as the publisher of the *Williams Lake Tribune*. His name was Stan. And as Stan rambled on about the newspaper, I tried to figure out how he'd found my name. He said something about my "impressive resumé," but I'd never sent a resumé to Williams Lake. I'd never heard of Williams Lake.

"Are you a student?" he asked.

I'd applied for enough summer jobs to know what he was really asking. "No, but I can pretend I am if it'll help you get a grant." After losing my chance to be an artistic director thanks to a lost government grant, it struck me as a fair trade.

"A man after my own heart," he said with a hearty chuckle.

Then he said something about "Quesnel," and I remembered a phone call I'd received months earlier from my friend, Neil. We'd worked together at the *Ubyssey*, the student newspaper at the University of British Columbia (UBC). Neil had asked whether I wanted to come work with him at a newspaper in Quesnel, and I'd politely declined. He told me to send my resumé just in case. I agreed just to humour him. But I didn't want to work for a newspaper. I didn't want to move to Quesnel.

I was going to be running a theatre company. Obviously the two papers were connected. Stan was vague on details, so I asked one of the essentials: "how much does it pay?"

"Between $1,100 and $1,200 a month. Depending on experience. Plus a 50-buck car allowance."

It wasn't going to help me spend Christmas in Maui, but $1,200 a month plus car allowance beat the heck out of six bucks an hour and free cookies. I'd interned at one of Vancouver's daily papers, the *Province*, I'd been published in some national magazines—I knew I'd get the top starting rate. I said I was interested.

"Okay, it's not my decision to do the hiring. You'll get a call from the editor sometime tomorrow. He'll let you know."

The editor called the next day. His name was Eric Something. He mumbled, so I wasn't sure what the something was.

"Do you like writing features?" he asked.

"Love it," I said. Writing features was my favourite part of journalism.

"Good, I need someone to work on a supplement we're putting out."

Supplement sounded interesting.

"Are you fast?"

"Very."

"Good, our last reporter was too slow." Then, the critical question. "How soon can you be here?"

"About a week if I leave now."

"Leave now."

"Great," I said. "So I start at $1,200, right?"

Pause. "$1,100."

"The publisher told me $1,200," I lied.

"He told me $1,100." I had no doubt he was lying too.

"He said between $1,100 and $1,200, depending on experience. I've got experience. And a degree in Creative Writing." I tried to sound like I wasn't budging for $1,100.

Another pause. Then: "$1,150. Plus car allowance." It sure sounded like a final offer.

Eric Something smelled blood. He knew I was out of work,

far from home and, if I was willing to move to a place called Williams Lake, I had to be desperate. There was a long silence at both ends of the phone. If I took the job I was probably being screwed, but if I didn't . . .

The words "Sorry, I won't work for less than $1,200" just wouldn't quite make it out of my mouth. "See you in a few days," I said.

Then Eric gave me his phone number and told me to call as soon as I got in. "Doesn't matter if it's two, three in the morning. Call any time. I'm looking forward to meeting you."

# Killer Bambis Attack City Slicker

////

W here the hell is Williams Lake?

It's probably a question I should have asked before I accepted the job. I knew it was near Quesnel, but I had no idea where Quesnel was either. I knew I should have looked Williams Lake up on a map before I stuffed everything back in my car and pointed it west, but that would have required thinking through a job offer that sent me driving over 3,000 miles to work as an underpaid reporter for a community newspaper in a community I'd never heard of. On the drive back it seemed like BC had moved further away—but maybe that was because I already had two speeding tickets. I'd always been convinced that all of Canada's 10 provinces were distinct until I drove through Manitoba and Saskatchewan and was so numbed by the lack of scenery that I was sure there were only nine provinces, plus Saskitoba. I picked up my third speeding ticket in Banff National Park. But as pretty as it was in Banff, it was hard not to speed. I was almost back in BC.

I waited until just after midnight on the fourth day of my cross-country drive to finally open a map. I waited until I was exhausted and hungry and, according to the map, only a few hundred kilometres away. Fortunately, before panic set in—I have a bad tendency to ignore maps and drive in the direction that looks most interesting—I spotted a sign at the side of the road, just on the outskirts of 100 Mile House. The sign said: WILLIAMS LAKE: 95 KILOMETRES.

So where the hell is 100 Mile House? And what exactly is it 100 miles from?

The answer to the second question, and, I guess, the first is Lillooet, which was mile zero on the Cariboo Wagon Road, the trail to the 1858 Cariboo gold rush—although if you didn't get the correct answer, I didn't know that little historical gold nugget at the time either. It was also 338 miles, 540 kilometres, and at least a hundred light years north of Vancouver.

A little footnote on the map declared that Williams Lake was part of the "Cariboo–Chilcotin region," which covered over 80,000 kilometres, stretching 650 kilometres from Bella Coola on Canada's west coast to the town of Likely in the centre of BC, and ranging from 70 Mile House (that would be 70 miles from Lillooet) north to Quesnel.

If I stepped on it, I figured I could make it to Williams Lake before 1:00 a.m., grab a bite to eat, check into a motel and collapse in a smelly heap.

Unfortunately, every time I tried to step on it I'd spot something that would slow me down. As a night owl, I knew there were plenty of road hazards for anyone driving after midnight. Half the cars on the streets between the witching hour and half-past closing time are driven by cops, cabbies or drunks. I'd seen flashers, junkies, street fights, wild wasted drivers spinning all over the road, and abandoned vans with no lights parked in the middle of highway lanes, but glowing green eyes were a new one on me—at least outside of a Stephen King movie. Glowing green eyes slowed me down.

I spun the radio dial and discovered there were only two stations. The CBC was playing classical music that would have knocked me out faster than any green-eyed monster could have, and the other station featured an evangelist saying something nice about Jesus. I was just checking out the Jesus station again when a set of green eyes darted across the road and I skidded to a stop.

That's when I saw that the horror-movie eyes belonged to cute, Bambi-like creatures, which made the prospect of hitting them even scarier.

About half an hour past 100 Mile House I spotted a forest fire. I pulled over and stepped outside the car—as soon as I made sure there were no green-eyed killer Bambis lurking in the bushes.

Once I was standing on the shoulder of the highway, I could see the fire was actually contained in a circle. I drove a little further on, saw another fire and stopped the car. Again. It was my first Unidentified Burning Object, and what confused me most about it was that it seemed to be burning above the treeline. The third UBO was close enough that I could finally see what it was. A volcano. It was shaped like a volcano and there was fire pouring out that had to be lava. I knew I probably would have heard if there were any active volcanoes in BC, but I didn't have any better theories. I thought it was beautiful, and if I'd had any idea how to make my dad's camera take pictures in the dark, I would have taken a shot or six.

I left my non-forest fire, evaded all remaining killer Bambis and, a bit after two, spotted another sign. It was like some huge wooden gift shop carving—the type someone's grandma has in the living room with her family name burnt into it. WELCOME TO WILLIAMS LAKE, it said. And below that: POPULATION 13,000. Thirteen thousand. That was less than half the population of the UBC campus.

I assumed Williams Lake was named after a White guy named William. I was wrong. I later discovered the place was named after a Shuswap chief who was named after a White guy named William.

I passed a couple of motels with their lights off, a gas station that had closed for the night, a gun shop and then a highway service artery, and finally my salvation—a 24-hour gas station and convenience store. I could buy some chips, ask the clerk which motel had the fewest rats and maybe, if I was really lucky, grab a copy of the paper I was going to write for.

As I pulled up, I noticed a trio of police cars parked by the side of the building. Typical. In Vancouver, if you had an emergency after midnight, your best bet would have been to call Bino's, a 24-hour coffee shop. In Toronto, some Tim Hortons should have hired staff sergeants to pour the coffee. In Williams Lake, the unofficial police HQ was obviously the Mohawk station off Highway 97.

I parked next to the cop cars and walked up to the door. A humourless silver-haired guy in a natty grey suit stopped me before I could step inside. "The store's closed for 10 minutes," he said. Then he pulled the glass doors shut and flicked the deadbolt.

Through the glass, between the signs announcing sales on pop, potato chips and cigarettes, I saw four other men standing in fairly official police poses. The silver-haired door keeper moved into the corner and started chatting up the clerk, notepad in hand. Brilliant observation of the evening: the cops weren't there for the coffee.

My journalist's killer instinct kicked in immediately. All the *Lou Grant* episodes I'd ever seen flashed before my eyes. Then they cut to the commercials, and I decided I was going to hop back in my dusty Toyota, search for a truck stop, order a greasy cheeseburger and a Coke, find a motel and pass out.

After 16 straight hours of driving I didn't want a news story. I wanted a bed. But looking back through the glass walls of the Mohawk station I was struck by something important. This was a small town. Robberies in small towns must be pretty rare. Not only that, all-night gas stations must be even rarer. I reached into my bag and grabbed some scrap paper and a pen.

I stood at the door until one of the uniformed cops came over and unlocked it. "We're closed," he said.

I didn't move. "This is going to sound strange," I said, "but I start work tomorrow as a reporter for the *Williams Lake Tribune*, and I was wondering if you could tell me what just happened here."

All the other cops suddenly stopped their chattering, and the one I was talking to—a pot-bellied redhead with a droopy walrus moustache—narrowed his eyes, twisted his lips into a sneer he must have practised back at the academy, and looked as if he was going to arrest me, beat me or alternate between the two until he got tired. "We'll have a press release in the book tomorrow. You can read that."

The other cops returned to their business, and the redhead—I heard the silver-haired dude call him Harvey—gave me his best "You are the scum of the earth" smirk before locking the door and turning away.

I probably would have left, if the cop hadn't smirked.

I went back and sat on the hood of my car. A few minutes later two cops walked outside. They were glaring at me so intently I half expected them to trip on the curb. They didn't. As soon as they drove off, I walked into the store. The three remaining cops stared at me like I was diseased. I cruised the aisles, ignored the glares, picked up a Coke and a copy of the *Williams Lake Tribune*, handed over a $2 bill and waited for my change. Then I asked to borrow the key to the washroom.

I read while I stood next to the sink. The *Williams Lake Tribune* was 24 pages, filled with lots of news about city hall, lumber mills, crafts fairs and local sports. It was my worst nightmare. I was about to start work as a newspaper reporter in a town with no news.

I had to talk to the clerk about the robbery because if this issue was any indication of what passed for excitement, a gas station holdup could be the biggest story of the year.

After about five minutes, I had read all the articles and started cruising the ads looking for interesting places to shop or eat. That was even more depressing than the stories. Other than discovering that I could score a Big Mac for $1.39, the local cuisine didn't look any more promising than the local news. On the bright side, if I wanted to settle down and buy a house it would cost less than $50,000.

After I'd killed about 10 minutes, I returned the key to the counter, went outside and walked past the gas pumps to the phone booth. Then I picked up the receiver and talked all about my drive—to the dial tone. Every so often I'd look up and smile at the scowling police officers as they stared at me through the sale signs and tried to figure out whether they could arrest me for being annoying. When the last of the patrol cars finally drove away I said farewell to the dial tone, went back to the store and asked the clerk what happened. I hate press releases.

The clerk was a fresh-faced young blonde with perfect 1970s bombshell hair—which still worked for her, even though it was 1985. She looked as composed as if she'd just spent the evening munching Jiffy Pop in front of the tube. "Hi," I said. "I start work tomorrow as a reporter for the *Williams Lake Tribune* and I was wondering if you could tell me what happened."

She did. First she told me her name and age. She was 21, a year younger than me. And her name was Tina Thurman. "That's Thurman with one R," she said. Then she reeled off the story of her holdup.

"Well, this guy comes in and he has a brown paper bag over his head with little eyeholes cut out. And he comes over to me and he takes out a knife and another brown paper bag. At first I thought he wants me to cut eyeholes in this new paper bag for him, and I reach for the knife but he pulls it back and says, "Gimme the money." So I gave him the money. That's our policy, never argue with robbers, right? Anyway, I'd just started my shift, so all he got was the float. Donna was here too. She'd just finished her shift, so she had a whole bunch of money in her purse, but he didn't ask about that. So I put all the cash register money in this paper bag of his and then he took off, and Donna called the police."

"You seem really calm," I said, thinking she was in shock. I was kind of surprised she'd kept the store open—or that a boss hadn't shown up to take over her shift. "You sure you're okay?"

"Oh yeah," she said.

"Do you think you're going to be able to keep working here after this?" I wasn't writing down the answer, just curious. Being robbed—even by a guy wearing a paper bag—had to be pretty traumatic.

"Well, when I first started here last month, I said if I ever got robbed I'd quit, but I don't think so now. After all, this is Williams Lake, you've got to expect these things. Don't put the bit in about me thinking he wanted me to cut eyeholes, okay. I'd feel stupid if you did that."

"No problem. How much money did he take?"

"You'd have to ask the police that."

"Okay, thanks." I was just about to go when it hit me that there was something strange about her story—something stranger than her thinking the guy with the knife just wanted her to cut eyeholes in the bag, or that this was her first robbery and she'd only worked here a month. I put my pen down.

"What do you mean you've got to expect these things?"

"We've got the highest crime rate in BC," Tina announced in a cheery voice with what sounded disturbingly like civic pride. "Everybody knows that."

"But an armed robbery in a town this size, that must be really rare." Front-page story with banner headline, was my guess.

When she started laughing, a hearty, very sane, jokes-on-you kind of laugh, I started to feel a little nervous. "Where are you from?"

"Vancouver."

"This is the second time this place has been robbed in the last two months." Then she began reeling off all the other violent incidents she could think of—shootings and robberies and dangerous barrooms where "you could get killed if you don't watch yourself." And after a few more minutes of sharing the type of anecdotes I would have expected from someone warning me off the toughest neighbourhoods in New York, she smiled cheerfully and chirped, "Welcome to Williams Lake!"

# Ace Photographer
# Exposed

///

When someone tells you to "call any time,"
they don't really mean, call any time. But Eric Something had
told me to "call any time."

I knew that calling at, say, five in the morning was bad form.
So after I stepped out of the Mohawk, I checked my watch. Since
it wasn't quite three, I figured I still had a margin of safety. I
never went to bed before three if I didn't have to.

So I returned to the booth and dialed Eric's number. After
Tina's tourist tips, I was wide awake and needed someone to talk
to and thought, just maybe, he'd offer me a place to sleep. I'd forgotten to ask Tina about a motel. Someone answered on the fifth
ring. I'd already decided to hang up at seven. I figure it's dangerous to talk to anybody at 2:45 a.m. after the seventh ring.

It was a woman on the other end. "Do you know what time it
is?" I was sure Eric Something was a man, and I was dreading
the possibility that this was one of those wrong numbers that
gets people out of bed at some ridiculous hour, usually on their
first day off in a month.

"I'm sorry," I said.

Then a sleepy male growled into the phone, "Who the hell is
this?"

"Is this Eric?"

"Yeah." I told him my name.

"So?"

"I'm your new reporter."

Eric sounded a bit happier—not much though—as he gave me the directions to his house. "See you in a few minutes," he grunted. This definitely beat finding a motel. I'd already spent half of my first month's salary driving to Williams Lake—and that wasn't counting the tickets. Just before he could hang up I told him, "By the way, I've got my first story."

Now he sounded awake. "What is it?"

"There was a robbery at the Mohawk station on Highway 97. I'll write it up for you tomorrow."

Eric laughed. "You really are a keener, aren't you?"

I'm not great with directions but, fortunately, Eric lived right down the hill from the Mohawk. He'd turned on the lights so I couldn't miss his house. He greeted me at the door. Looking just shy of 30, Eric was younger than he sounded on the phone and younger than I thought editors ought to be. He had a bushy brown moustache, wary eyes and looked like the guy who got shot for drawing an extra ace out of his sleeve in old westerns. He grunted, pointed me to the couch, told me we could talk in the morning and went back to bed.

The kitchen was next to the couch, and the next morning when I woke up, the woman who'd answered the phone was making tea and toasting bagels. "Hi, I'm Andrea," she said. Andrea was dressed in jeans and a peasant blouse, and I figured she was about my age. She looked very '60s, the type of pretty hippie chick guys buy funky clay pots or hand-crafted candles from at craft fairs, when they have no intention of ever using pots or candles. I was suddenly very aware that I wasn't wearing anything but my underpants, and pulled the sleeping bag up to cover my chest.

"Where's Eric?"

"Oh," she said, almost purring the next few words as she poured me a cup of tea. "He went to work hours ago."

My watch said it was barely nine. "Hours ago?"

"Eric likes to start around seven," she said. "Sometimes earlier." I didn't realize there was anything earlier than seven.

"Like the hair," she said.

And I realized my hair—which was a few inches past my shoulders—must look great after four days on the road. I ran my fingers through it to untangle it slightly. I started stammering something about needing a shower when she interrupted, "No, I like long hair." Then she grinned—a bratty grin—"and I'm sure Stan will love it. Want a bagel?"

I took that shower and then the bagel. As we drank our tea, Andrea started telling me all about Williams Lake. She'd clearly been talking to Tina, because the first thing she did was warn me about the crime rate. "Never leave your car door unlocked and never, never leave your valuables where people can see them. Ross, the guy you're replacing, left his camera on the front seat of his car, went into the *Trib* office to make a call and when he came back, the camera was gone and so was his windshield."

"How long was he gone?"

"Maybe two minutes."

I asked if she and Eric lived in a safe neighbourhood, and she said "safe" was a relative term. "We're heavily insured." Then she told me she'd heard plenty of great things about me. That sounded promising.

"Yeah, Eric says you're an ace photographer."

I almost coughed up my bagel.

"Eric had to choose between you and this girl from Edmonton. He liked the girl's resumé better—and she could have been here in a day—but he decided to go with you because Neil says you're such a hot photographer. Eric's a photographer too. He's won all sorts of photo awards."

Maybe I wouldn't need to waste money on insurance after all, but hopefully Neil had some because if I ever saw him again, I'd have to kill him. My photography experience pretty much consisted of taking vacation pictures with an Instamatic—many of which included stunning shots of an unidentified pink blob that turned out to be my index finger. I'd borrowed my dad's camera because I thought it would be fun to take pictures of all the amazing plays I'd be producing—but it was one of those scary things with lots of dials and more than one lens, and since I hadn't produced any plays I'd never even attempted to use it.

After we finished our bagels, we hopped in my car and Andrea navigated as we drove through downtown Williams Lake—all seven blocks of it—to the *Trib* building. Apparently I had the only car in town. Everyone else had a pickup—and every truck came equipped with a big dog and a gun rack. It was official. I had left Canada and entered one of those movies where guys who looked like me get tossed in jail by a redneck sheriff who calls him "boy."

The lake that gave the place its name was visible from pretty much everywhere and, for the most part, it was ringed by gravel roads, highway and endless rows of the types of large trees that people in BC tend to cut down and turn into money.

The main drag continued off the highway and narrowed into a quieter strip with a generic small-town mall anchored by a Woolco. This main street was criss-crossed by numbered streets. They numbered all the way up to seven. Just before we hit the numbered streets, the main drag became Oliver—home to a mix of offices, shops and restaurants with freshly minted Old-West theme-park facades.

As we drove, I told Andrea about my volcanoes. "Wood waste burners."

"They burn wood? Don't they sell all of it?"

"The burners cook the wood waste from the mills and the ash flies everywhere. Some days you'll wake up, look at your car and think it snowed. It's called 'fly ash.' That's why we have so many car washes in town," she said, gesturing to one on the corner. "There was a story in the paper last week calling for them to be banned. Environmentalists."

The newspaper office was cluttered, cramped and looked like the *Ubyssey* office, minus the empty beer bottles and roach clips. Every ancient wooden desk came complete with its own mess of papers, half-empty coffee mugs and overflowing ashtrays. A string of three offices lined the wall next to windows that faced a grocery store, where Eric sent me when I asked where I could grab a Coke. He also handed me a couple of two-dollar bills to pick up some cigarettes for him. (Almost everyone in the building smoked. My addiction was Coca-Cola—although on tight deadlines I also needed Dubble Bubble gum.) Beyond the store were the railroad tracks.

The offices had dividers between them, but the dividers seemed like afterthoughts, since they were only waist-high and there were large holes where there were supposed to be windows. "I didn't want windows," Eric told me. "I like to know what's going on. Make sure you're really working." Eric's office was in the middle of the room. He had the biggest, newest computer, a few shelves of reference books and In and Out baskets stuffed with enough paper to transcribe the encyclopedia in crayon.

I had the office in the corner to the left of his—an eight-by-eight-foot box with two desks, a whining computer terminal that somehow seemed ancient even in 1985, a heavily dented metal filing cabinet, shelves cluttered with yellowing newspapers, a comfy pink chair with foam leaking through the cracks in the vinyl, a typist's chair that creaked whenever I moved—and an editor lurking a few feet away.

The office on Eric's right belonged to the sports editor. Rick was 27, had a down-home drawl, and his office uniform consisted of jeans, a denim shirt and hand-tooled cowboy boots. He was clearly a local.

Next to Rick—in the main office—was a pretty 25-year-old woman with large owlish glasses and a cherubic face. Liz dressed smartly, but country smart. She was in charge of "community news," chronicling births, deaths, flower shows and science fairs—all the stories I knew I'd never read. She had the wonderfully contented smile of someone completely in charge of her own universe.

Across from Liz, at a series of desks covered with enough newspapers and notebooks to bury several bodies, was the storm at the centre of the calm. Abby was a big woman in her mid-30s with a shrill voice and the same mousy demeanor as Bugs Bunny's Tasmanian Devil. She was the other staff reporter, the "senior reporter," as she quickly informed me.

Everybody looked so busy, I wanted to be doing something too. When fingers weren't flying on keyboards they were diving for coffee mugs or scissoring cigarettes or all of the above. Even if they didn't have real news, it felt like a real newsroom.

"Write up your robbery," Eric suggested.

That killed about 15 minutes.

Then he told me who to call to get the weather report and showed me an example from a recent paper, so that I knew I was supposed to lead with a quip about whether to wear sunglasses, break out an umbrella or grab a toque. I suggested sunglasses before rattling off the Ministry of the Environment's sunny forecast. When I finished that in five minutes, Eric seemed more annoyed than pleased.

"We're very busy," he said as he clicked away on his keyboard, doing busy editor things.

I tidied my office, stared at my blank computer screen and, finally, decided it was close enough to noon to make a run for it and grab lunch.

I asked Abby if she wanted to come with me. I thought it would be nice to get to know the other reporter. "Nobody goes for lunch on production days," she said. "I'm the senior reporter here. I have responsibilities."

I asked Rick if he wanted to join me.

"You gotta be kidding," he said. "It's a production day."

Liz turned me down too.

So I picked up a stack of recent papers to find out exactly what wasn't going on in this town and went off on my own. I walked to a sandwich shop, flipped through the old *Tribs* and wondered if it wasn't too late to drive back to Ontario and learn to make cookies.

I found the column somebody'd written protesting the burners. According to the story, the average lot in Williams Lake caught 23 pounds of fly ash a month. The ash also wreaked havoc with the air quality, and I'm sure some lawyer someday will prove the debris was carcinogenic or hallucinogenic or otherwise toxic and sue the mills for millions. They were awfully pretty on a clear night, though.

When I got back, Eric took me downstairs to meet the publisher. Stan was as big as he'd sounded on the phone, kind of rugged too, but when he started to bluster, his bushy moustache made him look like he belonged in the Old West, running a railway and cursing the Hole-in-the-Wall Gang as they vamoosed with his loot. He ushered me into a faded leather chair in the corner of his office and looked me over like I was a sickly horse.

"We run a tight ship here," he said, trying to sound friendly but not quite pulling it off. "So keep your eye on the ball."

I wasn't sure how to respond, but I didn't have to. Stan was enjoying the speech much more than I was—even though I was sure he'd heard it before.

"You're going to have to write a lot, and don't be too proud to write business profiles. Remember," he said, getting to what was clearly the core of his philosophy, "advertising pays the freight around here."

Eric gave me a smile that I read as, "Ignore him, he's always like this." Eric was a man of few words but many smiles. Stan took me outside his office to introduce me to the sales staff.

"This is our new reporter," he announced. "If we knew what he looked like, we never woulda hired him." Then he chuckled unconvincingly.

Yup, Andrea was right. Stan loved the hair. I was obviously getting a haircut on my first day off.

Late in the afternoon, I was in my office sifting through more back issues of the *Tribune* when a blue-eyed, blonde pixie in painted-on blue jeans appeared from behind a door I'd hardly noticed because it was wallpapered with newspaper pages and black-and-white photos.

"You must be the new reporter," she said. "I'm Kate." Then, before I could introduce myself, she plucked my dad's Pentax off my desk. Kate was the staff photographer, and she was clearly keen on checking out the competition. As she rolled the camera around in her hands she paid careful attention to the buttons and levers I had yet to identify.

"Not bad," she said. "Abby has the same kind." I smiled, relieved. I had a good camera. Maybe it could take pictures without me.

"All rolls of film have to be in first thing in the morning. That's 8 a.m., 8:30 at the latest if you need them for that day's paper. Got it?"

I nodded, trying to picture being awake in time to deliver anything for 8 a.m.

"What kind of lenses have you got?"

Since I was pretty sure "glass" was the wrong answer, I shrugged. She gave me that leery Eastwood squint folks in cowboy country were obviously born with.

"You do have a flash, don't you?"

Flash. I knew what a flash was. It was one of those bulbs you put on the top of a camera to take pictures of people's red eyes at birthday parties. I checked the camera bag and rummaged through the various pockets while she watched, waiting for me to produce this mysterious device.

"I guess not," I finally said.

This was clearly the wrong answer.

"You'll have to buy one." Great, I was already spending more than I was earning. "Oh, and since I'm stuck in the darkroom all day I'm going to need you to take some mugshots later." She gave me all the details about the alderman I was supposed to photograph and where and when I'd find him. Then she started to leave.

"Can I ask a quick question?"

Kate turned around, scowling.

"Sure," she said, glaring at me like I'd just stolen her job. "But make it fast, I've got a batch of prints to do."

I picked up my dad's camera and shifted around so that my back was towards Eric before I whispered as softly as I could, "How do you load this thing?"

%

Just after five, when the paper had gone to bed, Abby asked where I was going to live, and I realized I had no idea.

"He can spend a few nights with us," said Eric. "Find a place on the weekend."

"There's a vacancy at that apartment on Third," said Kate.

"What about Sarah's place," suggested Abby. Then, before anyone could reply, she announced, "He should move in with Sarah."

"That's a great idea," said Kate.

Eric, Rick and Liz agreed. Before anyone even looked at me, Abby had already called the mysterious Sarah.

"Here," said Abby, handing me her phone.

"Uh, hi." I said.

"So you're the guy replacing Ross?"

"Yeah, I guess."

"You crazy?"

"Not particularly."

"You a psycho killer?"

"Not so far."

"Can you handle $225 a month?"

That was so much less than I was bracing to pay that she had to ask a second time before I said, "Sure."

"Great," she said. "I'll meetcha at the Billy after work. Bring your stuff. You can move in tonight." Then she gave me directions to the Billy Miner pub.

As I drove to meet my new roomie, I turned my radio on, hoping for more luck than I'd had the night before. The guy talking about Jesus had been replaced by a twanging guitar and Dolly Parton. This was pre-Shania, pre-Dixie Chicks, pre-Garth Brooks. I was a city kid. Other than the brief line-dancing epidemic caused by John Travolta and *Urban Cowboy*—something I thought might get him hauled before a war crimes tribunal— country music had not crossed over into urban pop culture, at least not for someone hooked on Springsteen and Seger car rock and campus radio. I flipped the dial and discovered that my only other choice was a CBC radio broadcast about crop conditions.

I kept spinning the dial, praying another station would emerge from the static. While the rest of the planet was listening to Madonna, Duran Duran and Bryan Adams, all I could find was The Judds singing "Mama He's Crazy." I settled on crop reports.

We all went for drinks at the Billy Miner after the paper went to bed. I didn't have to read the history lesson on the menu to know the bar was named after BC's most famous train robber, but there was nothing rough about the clientele. This was the bar the teachers and hospital workers hung out at after work. It was in a hotel, next to a Keg restaurant.

Sarah was a few years older than me and had a big grin and pouffy blonde TV hair. She was the reporter at the Judds and Jesus station. "The competition," said Abby, not sounding all that competitive.

"So you're my new roomie," she said, looking me over like I was on sale in a bargain bin. "You'll do." Then Sarah told me she was putting in her time in radio until she could get a TV job. It was the first thing she said after "You'll do."

Home was a duplex at the top of a steep gravel-covered hill. Beyond the hill all I could see was more hill covered with acres of forest. We had an ancient kitchen, a living room with a small TV and a fireplace. There was a porch with a glass door and swinging screen and beyond it, in the yard, a big metal garbage can. "What's that for?"

"It's our burn barrel."

Sarah looked at me like I was clueless. I looked back at her blankly.

"So the bears don't get the garbage."

Bears?

"When the bag's full, we toss it in the burn barrel."

I didn't ask, but she could see I was dying to.

"Then we burn it."

Cool. Our own personal wood-waste burner.

My room had a wooden floor, a closet, a bare bulb, a foam mattress and a window that looked out at our forest. It was perfect.

# Story Sparks Fire Fight

"**I**'m really angry with you."

It was 9 a.m., and I'm never truly conscious before noon, so it took a few seconds to place the voice on the phone. I was having enough trouble believing I was actually sitting at a desk this early. Since I'd only met five women so far and three of them were in the office, it didn't take me that long to figure this one out. It wasn't Andrea. It wasn't Sarah. Or Liz. Or Kate. It was Tina, the Mohawk clerk. "What's wrong?"

"Your story in the paper."

I opened the paper on my desk to my big scoop. Page six. Tina was obviously upset. She sounded scared, too. "Did I misquote you or something?" I'd never misquoted anyone before. Even the thought turned the chocolate Pop Tart in my stomach inside out.

"I didn't say you could quote me at all."

No, she hadn't, I thought. And I was starting to get nervous until I remembered the first thing she'd done after I'd started taking notes was spell her name for me.

"I told you you had to talk to the police."

That's right. She'd said that if I wanted to know how much money was taken, I had to talk to the police. I had talked to them, and they wouldn't tell me anything. Their press release consisted of "The Mohawk station on Highway 97 was robbed last night by a man with a weapon. No suspects at this time." No mention of money or knives or brown paper bags.

"I'm sorry if I caused you any trouble," I said.

"Well, the police just came and yelled at me. They said I shouldn't have talked to you at all, that now my name's in the paper the robber might come and track me down because I'm a witness."

I pictured Harvey, the cop with the walrus moustache, threatening her with tales of vengeful slashers and criminal conspiracies. But I took comfort in the thought that anyone whose idea of a disguise was a brown paper bag with eyeholes probably couldn't read. She yelled at me for another few minutes and then I apologized again.

"It's okay," she said at last, not sounding remotely sincere, then hung up.

I turned to Eric to confess through the big hole in the wall. I thought maybe I'd get fired. I'd pissed a lot of people off before—especially student politicians—but it was always the people my stories were supposed to piss off.

Here in Williams Lake I was batting a thousand.

"That's small-town journalism," said Eric. "Don't worry, once you meet Glenn, everything will be fine."

"Who's Glenn?"

"He's the staff sergeant, the local RCMP boss. Nicest guy in town."

Abby popped her head through the hole between Eric's office and mine. "He's right. Don't worry, kid, everybody loves Glenn."

"When can I meet Glenn?"

"This afternoon," said Eric. "I set up a meeting for you with the officer in charge of community policing. Glenn said he'd drop by." I was feeling better already. I'd meet Glenn. He'd straighten things out.

Then Eric asked me to do a short article to go with some pictures he'd shot the night before. He was driving home when he spotted a house burning down. Naturally, he pulled out his camera and started clicking away. He went through two rolls of film before asking the fire chief for details and finding out it was only "a practice fire." The house had been condemned and the department had permission to torch it so their volunteers—all but two of the firefighters were volunteers—could get some experience. So Eric wanted me to get enough info to piece together a story on volunteer firemen.

"The pictures are too good to toss," he said. "Besides, this'll be a perfect chance for you to get in good with the fire chief."

The fire department, the police station, city hall and the courthouse were all on the same block. And they were about a 10-minute walk from the *Trib* office. I drove. Since I didn't have any sense of direction—or any sense of which streets went one way and which ones turned into parks—it took 20 minutes to get there.

It turned out the fire chief wasn't around, but the assistant fire chief was. Reg Tallon stared at me like he was afraid I was going to spontaneously combust. "The police warned me about you," he said.

Warned him?

"They told me to watch out for you. But I'll give you the benefit of the doubt."

"Thanks," I said. I'd been in town less than two days and the police had already warned him about me? Good thing Glenn was going to straighten things out.

"Just promise me you won't publish the location of the practice fire. We don't want anyone getting any ideas that it's okay to start burning down those shacks. People sleep in some of those places. Someone could get hurt."

"I don't even know where the fire was," I said.

Reg still looked wary.

"I don't know where anything is. I don't even know what street we're on now."

That seemed to do the trick. I opened my clipboard and started writing as Reg told me all about the brave volunteer firemen aiming their hoses at the flaming shack.

A few hours later I walked back to city hall for a "media briefing" on community policing. The rest of the media was already there.

"Hi, Sarah."

"Hi, Mark."

The designated community liaison officer was Constable Bob Terry, a fast-talking plainclothes cop who seemed like he'd be more at home in a stock exchange than a squad car. Constable Bob was surprised Sarah and I had already met.

"Met," said Sarah. "We're already living together." That scored a raised eyebrow.

I asked Constable Bob why he'd chosen to work in Williams Lake, and he explained that once you joined the RCMP they decided where you were posted. He was from Toronto, and although he'd been around over a year he had definitely not gone native. Bob spent about 20 minutes outlining his goals for community projects, explaining that the key to all this was good relations with the media. Then the door opened.

Glenn looked just like Eric and Abby said he would: friendly, paternal, cuddly—but they'd left out the Jack-Nicholson-in-*The-Shining* homicidal gleam in his eyes.

Glenn cheerfully greeted Bob, hugged Sarah, then turned to me. "So you're the new guy from the *Tribune*. I'm Staff Sergeant O'Donnell." I put out my hand to shake his. He let my hand hover in the air. Fortunately, he wasn't armed or I might have run for the door, jumped in my car and left town without bothering to pack.

Bob returned to his regularly scheduled speech, but the sergeant wasn't interested in community policing. As soon as Bob paused for breath, O'Donnell started talking about ethics. Or lack of ethics.

"That girl said she didn't even agree to be interviewed."

"She lied," I said, "because one of your officers went and scared the hell out of her."

"I don't know what kind of reporting you did in the city, but this kind of attitude won't play in a small town like Williams Lake." Then he paused before adding, "We won't put up with it." At least he didn't call me "boy." But I was pretty sure he thought it.

So much for police–media relations. I went back to the office to tell Eric and Abby that Glenn might not love everybody after all.

I phoned Barb that night to tell her about my first shift. She suggested I should pack the car and drive home. "I can't just quit," I said.

"Why not?"

"I just got here."

Fortunately, I didn't have much time to dwell on my problems with the RCMP. The next day, while I was walking to the courthouse to cover my first trial, I saw Reg watering the fire-hall lawn. I waved at my only official friend, and he looked ready to strangle me with his hose. "I told you not to print that address," he said, sounding like somebody had accidentally given him decaf for breakfast.

"I didn't."

"Well, what's it doing in the paper then?"

"It's not in the paper. I wrote the story and I don't even know the address."

"It's in the story," Reg said firmly.

I hadn't seen the paper yet, but I knew what I hadn't written.

"I don't have any idea where those shacks are. So I know it's not in there. I swear—"

Then it hit me. Eric must have thought I'd left the address out because, being new to town, I didn't know it. It had never occurred to me to tell Eric I'd been ordered not to reveal the location of the fires. I'd had editors cut stuff in my stories before, but I couldn't ever remember them adding anything. I tried to explain this to Reg, but he wasn't buying it.

"Glenn was right about you. If one of those houses gets torched, if anybody dies, it's on your head." And he glared at me like I'd already killed somebody.

"I'm sorry."

"Well, you'd better shape up," he said. Then he looked away from me and went back to his gardening. I crossed the street to the courthouse, wondering who I was going to offend next.

# *Practice Fires*
# *Make Perfect*

I'm not sure how I did it, but for the next few days I somehow managed to stay out of trouble. All I wrote were the type of stories I assumed small-town journalists normally covered.

Eric announced that my official beats were crime, the environment, labour, forest fires, Native affairs, education and anything else he could think of. I preferred Abby's explanation. "I cover local politics, you cover everything else. Stay away from city hall. That's my beat."

"Everything else" meant Abby still wrote about two-thirds of the news in every paper.

Every morning at a little after 9, I'd appear at the RCMP station and ask for the press book so I could read the day's so-called press releases to find out who hurt who the night before. The "press releases" were one-line blurbs grudgingly filled out by the duty officer at the end of his shift, stating the crime committed, and no further details, in a ledger (I am not being sexist when I say "his"—there were no "shes" with badges in Williams Lake.) If I wanted more information, I had to hope someone at the front desk was in a good mood. When the secretaries stalled, I'd wait. If the story was worth it, I'd ask to speak to Staff Sergeant O'Donnell. If he was "busy," I'd lean on the counter until he poked his head out the door so I could try and get a bit more than "A robbery occurred at the Dog 'n' Suds last night. A quantity of money was taken. No suspects."

Because of my penchant for waiting until someone told me at least some of what I wanted to know, I developed a reputation as a pest. I cultivated the reputation. It cut down on my waiting time.

After the police were done ignoring me, I'd walk over to the courthouse to see what trials were on deck. Since no one was willing to tell me, I had to learn to translate the numbers that corresponded to each crime. There were two courtrooms—a small one on the first floor and a large one on the second. Each had a list posted outside the door that looked like a set of hockey statistics. The court clerk's office had a secret decoder ring that explained which numbers added up to what crime.

The next stop was the Ministry of the Environment (to check for forest fires) and the fire department (to check for house fires). I usually arrived at the office by 10 (unless there was a particularly interesting trial to cover) and did a few more routine checks by phone. I'd get the weather report from real, live meteorologists, and once every week I'd find out what was happening with the town's biggest hero—and arguably Canada's too—Rick Hansen. When Hansen was 15 he'd caught a lift home from a fishing trip. He and his friend rode in the back of the pickup, like typical Cariboo teenagers. The pickup skidded out of control, Hansen flew out of the cab and almost died. On March 21, less than two months before I arrived in Williams Lake, the now paraplegic Hansen, inspired by the memory of his friend Terry Fox, had set off to attempt a wheelchair journey around the world to raise money for spinal-cord research. Once a week I'd call his sister to find out where he was. When I arrived in Williams Lake, Hansen was still in North America.

Then I'd take off for lunch—hitting Gringo's for something kind of like tacos, the deli for sandwiches or the Dog 'n' Suds for Coney burgers. Kate introduced me to Coney burgers on a non-production day. Dog 'n' Suds was straight out of *American Graffiti*. The only thing missing were the waitresses on roller skates. The place had McDonald's thin fries, thinner burgers, creamy coleslaw and, if you had to guess, you'd figure it would go under the day a McDonald's rolled into town. But even after a McDonald's materialized next door, the Dog 'n' Suds was still the busiest place in town. I'm convinced it was because of the Coney sauce, a sweet-spicy, chunky and totally addictive chili mix. There actually were some fine-ish dining establishments in Williams Lake, and the Chinese–Canadian restaurant you can find in every Canadian small town, right next to Tim Hortons. But I think the only true indigenous cuisine was Coney sauce, which you could order on burgers or fries and was so addictive I can still taste it as I write this.

On production days I'd eat alone. No one else left their desks.

After lunch I'd work on features, follow up on news leads and chase after Eric's tips. In my first few weeks on the job, the "everything else" beat included a nine-year-old girl who won a no-carat diamond ring for her mother in a jewellery store promotion. A cookie factory full of Girl Guides, Cadets and Brownies—2,200 of them—descended on the park in McLeese Lake for a 75th anniversary celebration. And a controversy broke out at the nearby Anahim Lake Stampede. Some of the locals were outraged that government busybodies were suggesting spectators should no longer be allowed to sit on the top rail of the rodeo ring. (Yes, that would be the same rodeo ring where wild bulls ran loose. Sitting somewhere they couldn't get killed made the local fans feel like sissies.)

The police gave me a heads-up about bear sightings. Some locals had caught bears playing in gardens and digging through their garbage. Since I knew my garbage can was bear bait, I paid special attention when a forestry official explained that if you meet a bear, "Don't panic, just turn and walk away," which seemed like good advice for most situations in Williams Lake.

And Kate taught me how to take pictures. Sort of.

The trick—in case you're wondering how this was done in the days before point, click and fix in Photoshop—is to make sure you don't aim into the sun, don't point the flash at people's eyes, watch out for reflective surfaces and set the little dial to 800 for 400 ASA film, so it will all be slightly overexposed. That way anything that doesn't work can get fixed in the darkroom by your new best friend Kate. "And take as many shots as possible," she told me while we hid from Eric in the darkroom. "One of them's bound to turn out okay." Actually, a lot of them did. Although I had no idea what any of the dials on my camera meant, Kate said I had a good sense of composition and whatever I got wrong technically, she fixed.

So if Eric noticed I wasn't the ace photographer he'd hoped for, he didn't complain. Eric wasn't Lou Grant, but he'd cultivated that classic cynicism they teach in editor school. His voice was caustic enough that he almost always sounded annoyed— even when he was laughing. And he laughed a lot the day he announced that Stan wanted to take me to lunch. It was my third week, and I still hadn't convinced any of the other reporters to eat with me on a production day, but somebody went for lunch. Our boss. There was a Kiwanis meeting, and Stan said this would be a good chance to meet "the important people in the community."

We got into Stan's Jeep and drove past the Mohawk station to the Bil Nor, one of the two Chinese restaurants. I was sure a letter or three must have gone missing from the sign at some point, but the name never changed.

The important people looked exactly how I expected the important people to look—middle-aged men in crisp, off-the-rack suits, who seemed to take themselves very seriously—at least at Kiwanis lunches. The best part of lunch was the drive back, when I asked Stan what a publisher does for a living. There's an art to asking a rude question like that and getting away with it. It helps to look as innocent as possible, or as Nancy—my very blonde editor at the *Ubyssey*—used to call it, my dumb-blonde routine. Genuine curiosity never hurts either. And that was sort of the case here. I really wasn't sure what publishers did, besides bother editors. Student newspapers don't really have publishers and I'd never dealt with one as a freelancer.

Stan was flustered, but when he saw that I meant it—or at least looked like I meant it—he explained that a publisher's job was to run the business end of a paper. "The problem with Ma and

Pa operations is that Ma and Pa may love to write, but neither of them have the time or interest to sell ads and watch the cash flow." Then Stan told me he'd helped take over a few Ma and Pa operations, and that's how his chain now included almost two dozen newspapers. "I don't know anything about journalism," he boasted, "but I know how to make a profit."

The journalist in me was disturbed, but the realist knew if I ever started a business, I wanted Stan around to watch that cash flow.

After my big lunch, I did a two-page feature on the nobility of auxiliary police officers—volunteers who got to wear the uniform for special events. The day after that was published, Glenn almost smiled at me as he said, "Nice job."

That night I decided to call Barb to tell her I was finally settling in. Unfortunately, I didn't have a phone yet—the phone had been in Sarah's ex-roomie's name and was disconnected when he left. So I had to drive to the bus depot, since long-distance calls from work were verboten and not very private.

I was just telling Barb how the powers-that-be seemed ready to accept me when our conversation was interrupted by the screech of car tires and a nasty thud at the city's main intersection, where the two highways met.

I'd already started driving towards the accident when I realized my camera was at home, so I pulled a U-turn and whipped along a side street at 80 kmh. I had driven a few blocks when I had to slow down to get past a crowd. About a dozen people were standing on the street gawking as the fire department tried to rescue a blazing house. Another scoop.

Once I passed the crowd I floored it, blithely ignoring stop signs and oncoming pickups with big dogs in the back. I skidded into our driveway, sprinted into the house, grabbed my camera and raced back to the fire, pulling onto someone's front lawn to park. I'd been snapping away and not aiming into the sun or at reflective surfaces for about five minutes before Reg came over and said, "You do know this is a practice fire, don't you?"

Shit.

I ran back to my car, raced to the intersection and hoped the mess—which definitely was not a practice accident—was still there. It was. A fire beat a car accident, but a car accident aced a practice fire.

A pickup had collided with a motorcycle. The motorcycle had been reduced to spare tires held together by scrap metal. The pickup may have been scratched, but I couldn't tell. A crowd of surly bikers and elderly cowboys had gathered to stare and make the same kind of murmuring rhubarb noises as movie extras. The investigating officer was snapping photos, so I looked for witnesses. A biker told me the guy driving the motorcycle was okay—the ambulance driver had told him it looked like a broken leg—but it was all the other guy's fault. The truck made an illegal turn, said the biker. I knew Glenn would kill me if I quoted a guy with a motorcycle about a motorcycle accident, so I turned to a friendly-looking, 50ish cowboy, took his name and asked what he'd seen.

"Well, the guy on the motorcycle was thrown a few feet, but he seemed to be okay. Tried to make a turn and didn't see him."

"The truck driver did?"

"Yeah."

"And where were you at the time of the accident?"

"Driving the truck."

And that's when Harvey showed up. I think the bristles of his walrus moustache actually stood up as he shot me a look that could have melted the remains of that motorcycle.

He told the driver that he shouldn't be talking to me, and I figured I'd take the opportunity to make amends. "I'll come by the station to get the details from you tomorrow," I suggested, trying to sound as ingenuous as possible. Harvey grunted and led the driver away.

I drove to the *Trib*, wrote up the story, then got back in my car to head home. It was around eleven—three hours after the accident and the fire—and instead of taking my usual route, I decided I'd hit the Mohawk station and grab a Coke—as long as Tina Thurman with one "r" would sell me one. And that's what I was doing when I spotted two fire engines and three police cars in front of the town's only shopping mall. There was smoke floating out of the main doors. This was not a practice fire.

The police and firemen were inside the mall. I would have joined them, but it occurred to me that, if I did, the police might "accidentally" shoot me. So I took out my pen, my notebook and my camera, perched on the hood of my Toyota and waited. I was still waiting as another police car pulled into the lot. When I saw who it was, I grinned my best Cheshire Cat grin and waved like it was my party and I was glad he could make it.

I suspect it must have taken all of Harvey's self-control not to shoot me.

I found out the next day that someone had ripped off the sporting goods store and set the fire to cover their escape. All alone in the mall, and he'd stolen about a hundred bucks worth of sports gear. That was his big haul. The guy was clearly related to the criminal mastermind who'd robbed the Mohawk. There was some smoke damage to the sports shop, but the rest of the mall was fine.

I told Eric about my big night out and that I was a little worried. The closest I'd ever been to trouble with the police was a warning I got when I was 14. "Don't jaywalk," the cop had said. That was it. I hadn't even been called to the principal's office since grade nine.

"Don't worry," said Eric, "I've got good news. I talked to Glenn about you the other night when I was at the regimental ball."

"That's great," I said, truly relieved.

"Yeah," said Eric. "He thinks you have your very own police radio scanner and that you're a sleazy big city reporter who doesn't belong in a small town and he doesn't trust you one bit."

This was good news?

Eric smiled sweetly. "I told him to give you a chance."

"So they really do hate me?"

"You make them real nervous," he said, and his smile shifted back into a wicked grin. "I like that."

# Teen Journalist
# Tells All

%%

I made the cops nervous. My editors at the *Ubyssey* would have been so proud. For a student journalist, the only thing better than pissing off the police would be bringing down a politician. But I didn't write to piss people off—even if that did sometimes seem to be my specialty. I wrote because it's all I'd ever wanted to do. I may have arrived in Williams Lake by accident, but there was nothing accidental about becoming a journalist. Writing was always my plan.

When I revealed that to my high-school family studies teacher, she asked what my backup plan was. I said I didn't have one. "That's not very *realistic*," she said, with an italic sneer on the word "*realistic*." When I shrugged a standard-issue 16-year-old shrug, she launched into her patented responsibility riff.

"Not many people make a living as writers. What about law? Or teaching? Have you ever thought about teaching?" Maybe teaching family studies, I thought, so I could learn how to crush students' dreams? Then she gave our class an assignment to catalogue our career options. "You have to include a Plan B," she said, staring at me when she said it. For Plan B, I wrote: "Starve."

That wasn't entirely true. I had two passions—writing and theatre. But if my family studies teacher thought I was unrealistic, she thought my friend who wanted to be an actress was certifiable.

I'd loved writing stories since elementary school, and then, in grade ten, I discovered journalism, pretty much by accident. In grade nine I had a huge crush on Sandee, a girl I'd worshipped since elementary school. Sandee wanted to be friends, so anyone over the age of 14 knows the romantic part of this story won't end well. In order to spend time with Sandee, who was taking a class at summer school, I signed up for it too. It was the perfect course for an English whiz like me. Advanced math. I took a full year of math in six weeks. Only God knows why I didn't behave like a normal lovestruck teen geek and pick up an electric guitar. Or at least get into drugs. Since I spent all my time in math daydreaming about Sandee, I have no idea how I passed. And that meant that when I entered grade ten, I was in grade eleven math.

When I saw the blackboard on the first day of class, I knew I was in the wrong place. Those symbols couldn't have anything to do with math. Those symbols had to be Latin. No, I was pretty sure I'd recognize Latin. They were clearly extraterrestrial.

The grade eleven math teacher, Mr. Murphy, looked and sounded exactly like a Mr. Murphy should. He was in his mid-50s, dressed in tweeds and had an accent like the Lucky Charms leprechaun. The first time Mr. Murphy spoke to me was two weeks into class, when he handed back my first quiz—which carried a grade so low, only an advanced algebra whiz could have calculated it.

"You really don't understand a word of this, do you, son?"

"No, sir, " I said. "I don't." It was the only time I had ever called a teacher "sir." But it was also the only time it had ever crossed my mind that there was a grade lower than F. Mr. Murphy nodded.

"Stick around after class."

I wondered if it was possible to get thrown out of school for failing a quiz. But once the classroom cleared, Mr. Murphy had a better idea. "Would you like to see if we can transfer you to a different class?"

I didn't say "sir" this time. I didn't say anything. I just nodded. If I'd said anything I'm sure I would have started crying.

"What are you good at, son?" Before I could answer, Mr. Murphy flashed his leprechaun smile. "I know it's not math."

"English," I said. "I really like English."

"Good," he said, "I've called the guidance counsellor's office to see what else we could get you into." He'd already checked the schedule? He obviously wanted me gone as badly as I wanted out. "How do you feel about journalism?"

I followed Mr. Murphy up to the third floor to find the journalism teacher. Ms. Malloy was a pale, brittle woman who already looked burnt-out just two weeks into the school year. Mr. Murphy asked me to stay back, and I did, but I was close enough to hear the tail end of their conversation. Ms. Malloy was loud enough that everyone in the hall probably heard it.

"My class is already overcrowded. I've got 32 kids. I only have room for 30."

"But he really wants to take journalism."

I did?

"No way. I'm sorry."

"Please, Shelley, it would be a personal favour. I'd owe you."

I loved this man.

"The last thing I need is another stupid kid taking this course because he thinks it'll be an easy pass." I'd never heard a teacher refer to students as "stupid" before. Mr. Murphy looked like he was staring Ms. Malloy straight in the eyes, even though his eyes barely reached her neck.

"He'll get an A," he said.

I'd what?

"He'll be your best student," he said. "I guarantee it."

Ms. Malloy stared right back at him. "No."

A week and one more humiliating math quiz later, Ms. Malloy went on stress leave. Mr. Murphy begged a favour from the counsellor and slipped me into the class, hoping the sub wouldn't complain. Before I went in, he informed me, "You're getting an A."

I promised I would. So on my first day of class, when the sub asked for volunteers to intern at the *Vancouver Courier* for extra credit, my hand shot up. By the time Ms. Malloy returned a month later to discover she now had 33 students, my first assignment was the lead story in the class paper, and I'd already published an article in the *Courier*. That term I wrote five more stories for the *Courier* and had the lead feature in both editions of the class paper. The first person who saw my report card that year was Mr. Murphy. I got his A.

The next year I joined the school's student paper, and the year after that, I took over as editor and started writing features about whatever I knew we weren't allowed to write about. *Lou Grant*, a series about life at a fictional LA daily, was on TV, and my hero was Rossi, Lou Grant's version of Carl Bernstein. (Despite the character's Italian name, the actor, Robert Walden, was way too Jewish to be a Bob Woodward.) I loved the idea of a reporter who only wrote things his editor and publisher told him not to. I loved the idea of interviewing people, finding out what was really going on, before anyone else did. My other journalistic hero was Carl Kolchak, *The Night Stalker*. But while I wrote a few cool ghost stories—and was once invited to spend Halloween night in a graveyard with a group of Satanists—I never did kill any vampires. At least none I'm willing to admit to.

My first front-page feature for the student paper was on teen suicide. In our second issue, I put together an exposé of a teacher who'd slapped a student. When our staff sponsor told us we couldn't run it, I told her I would pay for the printing myself with our ad revenue, and we'd distribute the paper off school property. Our sponsor took me aside to explain that the teacher in question had been suspended, was on the verge of a nervous breakdown and she was afraid my article might put him over the edge. She also told me that if I ever revealed what she'd said, she'd be fired faster than I could spell "Rossi." It was the only story I ever spiked.

In my final year of high school, I applied to the creative writing programs at UBC and UVic. I didn't want to go to university, but I couldn't imagine any newspaper hiring me on the strength of my experience at a high school paper and my encyclopedic knowledge of *Lou Grant* and *The Night Stalker*. So why disappoint the parents who'd agreed to pay my tuition in the hopes I'd become a lawyer?

I was accepted into both schools, but I wasn't sure I wanted to accept UBC. The creative writing program didn't include journalism, which seemed to be the only way writers could actually make a living. Going to UVic meant I could study journalism, live away from home and, since this was the last of Canada's hippie universities, there were no science, language or, best of all, math requirements to get an arts degree. But the most exciting thing about UVic was the news I got from my friend Bob, who was in first year there. He assured me that not only was the campus great, but that if a guy lived in residence, he would most definitely meet a girl who would have sex with him. UVic sounded very appealing.

I figured there was only one way to decide which university I should attend. Since Bob had already spent a year in university and I looked 12, I asked him if he'd visit the student papers with me.

We went to UBC first. I had no idea then that the student paper, the *Ubyssey*, was the launching pad for some of Canada's most famous journalists (including two of my heroes, Alan Fotheringham and Eric Nicol). All I knew was that the paper came out three times a week.

The office looked like it had just been robbed, and smelled like stale beer and fresh dope. The first person I met when I walked in the door—the only person in the room—looked like Zonker from *Doonesbury*, only not quite as well-drawn. There was an open beer bottle on his desk. It wasn't quite 11 a.m. Toto was definitely not in high school anymore. Before I could tell Zonker I wanted to join the paper, he was already ranting. "You're a first year, aren't you? A fuckin' first year." He hadn't even bothered to look up from his typewriter.

"I hate first years," said Zonker. "They were all stars at their high school paper, and none of them can write for shit. You know what'll happen to you if you come here." It wasn't a question.

"You'll be lucky if you get a byline before you're in second year. If you last that long. And you won't. Know why? Because if a story gets rewritten you don't get a fuckin' byline. And every story by every first year gets rewritten 'cause none of you can fuckin' write and none of you should even be fuckin' graduating from high school. Never mind graduating with fuckin' A averages."

He took a gulp of the beer and finally looked up at me and glared at Bob. Then he went back to hammering the keys on his IBM Selectric. He was not as mellow as the real Zonker.

"Uh, thanks," I said. Bob glared back at him. I was a gangly geek. Bob was a jock. Bob wanted to beat the shit out of him.

The next week I took the ferry to Vancouver Island and drove to UVic. After Bob showed me the Student Union Building, I walked into the office of the *Martlet* alone. I couldn't risk Bob killing an editor on his home campus. The editor didn't look at all like Zonker. He looked more like . . . Snoopy.

"I'd like to join the paper next year," I said.

"Do you have any experience?" he asked politely.

I told him about my high school paper and the stories I'd written for the *Courier*.

"Wow," he said.

He said "wow" the way "Zonker" said "fuck," and used the word just as liberally.

"Wow. Would you like to be an editor?"

There were no beer bottles in this office and it smelled like Lemon Pledge. Everything was tidy enough that it would have easily passed a snap inspection by a committee of moms.

"We have sub-editors here and we pay them. Not much. Just $40 a week. But with your experience, I'm sure you could be a sub-editor. And next year—wow—maybe by next year you could be editor."

I spent almost an hour in the *Martlet* office while Snoopy told me all about his paper and how much fun it was to work there. "Wow" was right.

By the time I got back to Bob's dorm room, I knew where I had to go. I told Bob.

"Are you out of your mind?"

"They want to make me an editor," I said.

"And pay you," he said.

"Yup."

"And you want to go to UBC! Are you out of your mind?"

"They already think I'm good enough to be an editor here. How am I supposed to learn anything?"

※

I did get a byline on my first story for the *Ubyssey*. The story was edited—but it wasn't rewritten. I covered a speech by an environmental activist who'd discovered that in the 1950s, the university had dumped barrels of radioactive material into the water off campus. The headline was "UBC Radioactive Dumping Dumped On."

It turned out Zonker was the editor, but it was the sub-editors—especially Nancy, an agriculture student built like a basketball player, who taught me how to write and research a news story, how to properly attribute a quote and how to avoid getting sued.

My most infamous article saved every student at the university $10 a year. The Student Union had instituted a special levy to upgrade the Student Union Building (SUB). The referendum failed, but the levy was like income tax, the student politicians had no plans to revoke it. Nancy suggested I challenge them on it. I did. I interviewed the student-council president and kept innocently rephrasing the same question: "When will you get rid of the levy?"

She kept repeating variations on the same answer. Some day the students would vote for the renovations and the money would come in handy.

"So you're not going to give it back?"

"No," she said.

"Never?" I asked.

"The renovations will happen. It's just a matter of time."

"So never then?"

"We're not giving it back," she said.

I smiled sweetly, thanked her for her time, went back to the office and wrote my lead. "The UBC president says she's not giving students their building fund money back until SUB freezes over."

When the paper came out the next day, the president called me into her office. Nancy had already told me what I was supposed to do. I went into the president's office and, as soon as she stopped screaming at me, told her my editor had completely rewritten my story.

"That's what editors are for," Nancy had told me. "That way you can interview her tomorrow when she announces she's giving the money back." And I did.

In second year, Nancy became my official editor and I became one of her lead reporters—in part because so many of the paper's stars were moonlighting with jobs in the professional media. Out of two dozen regular contributors to the *Ubyssey*, six were working part-time for the city's leading daily, the *Vancouver Sun*, another eight worked part-time for community papers, and just after Christmas I scored a job at the city's other daily, the *Province*.

The first day at the *Province*, my editor, Al Stevenson, showed me around. Stevenson was gruff, grizzled, bearded and bitter— and I don't know if he was a chain-smoking heavy drinker, but I hope so, because that would have made him the perfect *Front Page* cliché. Stevenson showed me a wall of little wooden boxes stuffed with press releases, messages, memos and—most importantly—tiny pink slips of paper.

Each slip had a story idea on it. Then Stevenson pointed out my box, which was labelled "Intern Two," and told me that every Monday when I showed up for work I'd find my assignment on one of those pink slips. Since I'd get all the information on the slip, no editor would ever have to be troubled by actually talking to a lowly intern.

My first slip told me I had to write an obituary for a former chancellor of UBC. I was terrified. Summing up someone's life in a few hundred words was a job I thought called out for a senior writer, someone with context and a sense of the poor man's history. If these were the last words the man's friends and family would ever read about him, I had to make sure they were the best words I'd ever written. I went to the newspaper archives and asked for everything they had on the deceased. That was when I discovered my editor had made a huge mistake. This guy was still alive!

Stevenson was at his computer when I ran over with the big news. He looked at me like I'd just peed on his carpet. "Of course he's still alive. But he's old. We do these so we've got something on file for when the guy does die."

I said, "Okay," but I thought, "Creepy." The obituary I wrote didn't end up running for almost 10 years, so I hope some intern took the trouble to update it.

The following Monday I looked in my box and saw four pink slips. I wanted to run, I wanted to cry, I wanted to plead with Stevenson to cut me some slack. After all, I was just an intern. I'd never written more than one story in a day. I couldn't imagine a writer switching gears so quickly. Maybe I could do two—but four? I looked at Stevenson slouched over his keyboard like a wild, um, editor. And I knew that if I asked him about this— especially after thinking obituaries were just for dead people— my journalism career was over. I had no choice. I had to write the stories. I didn't break for lunch. I didn't break for snacks. I didn't break to breathe. By the end of my shift, I turned in four stories.

The next week there were *six* pink slips in my box.

This was my routine for the next three months. After I'd finished the assignments in my box, Stevenson usually told me to work a few hours of overtime to write another story or two. That's how I finally met "Intern One," a Langara student named Cindy who worked the other shift. On one of my rare Coke breaks, she asked how I was liking the job.

"It's pretty exhausting," I said. "I never imagined I could write so much so quickly."

"Me neither," said Cindy. "I don't think it's fair they expect us to write a whole story every shift."

I was sure I'd heard her wrong. "A story? You write one story?"

"Yeah," said Cindy indignantly. "My journalism instructor always gives us a week."

I was almost as shocked at the idea of a journalism instructor teaching students they could take a week to write a news story as I was at . . . "ONE STORY?"

Cindy was getting progressively more outraged. "I know. It's terrible! We should say something. Do you want to say something?"

I couldn't say a word. I just held up my collection of pink slips. I had seven that day.

"Exactly," she said. "And how are we supposed to choose? That's not fair either." She looked at my slips, studied them a moment, shrugged. "I guess they give you all the ones I don't do, in case you're interested in them. I didn't like those ones."

I just heard one word. "CHOOSE?"

"Yeah. Mr. Stevenson said that each week I was supposed to choose the story I thought I could do best, but I'm never sure. How do you choose yours?"

Choose?

No wonder I was scoring so much overtime. The previous week I'd written five stories that covered almost every inch of pages four and five of the *Province*. I'd been told that the reason my byline was only on one of the stories was newspaper policy. Years later I realized that having five stories in the paper by one student intern would have sparked a helluva union grievance.

I probably should have felt exploited, but when Stevenson urged me to apply for a summer job, I began reimagining my future instead. Maybe I wouldn't have to go back to university. I'd only wanted a degree because I thought it might help me make a living as a writer, and here was my big chance. My life was set, and then . . . Stevenson offered me another overtime shift. I was thrilled. Until he said: "I want you to do a Clifford Olsen story."

Before I even had time to think about it, the word was out of my mouth: "No."

"What do you mean, no?"

"I don't want to do a Clifford Olsen story."

Stevenson looked as if I'd told him the sky was green and grass was blue. Reporters aren't supposed to say "no" to editors, especially intern reporters who have just been urged to apply for a summer job, especially when the reporter is being asked to follow up the biggest story of the year, maybe the decade—a serial killer who was convicted of brutalizing and murdering at least 10 children, after he'd sold the police the locations of his victims' bodies for $10,000 apiece.

"Why not?"

I realized I was committing journalistic treason, but it was too late to back down. When he'd said "Olsen," the image that ran through my head was of phoning one of the victim's parents and asking some inane question about how they felt, in the hopes that they'd burst into tears. I didn't care if it meant my job, or my future career, I was not going to phone a grieving parent for a quote.

"Because," I said, knowing these were my last words as a *Province* employee, "I think the coverage of Clifford Olsen has been sensationalized to the point where it's obscene and . . . "

And that's when Stevenson stuck his fingers in his ears and started to hum. It was something my brother David did once . . . when he was six. I stopped talking and started laughing.

Stevenson pulled his fingers out of his ears and stopped humming.

"I will take that from members of the public, but I will not take that from members of my own staff."

I was stunned to hear I was still on staff. Then he told me the assignment was a simple "match," the polite journalistic term for creatively plagiarizing someone else's work. In this case, the story was from a TV news piece in which Olsen's wife announced she was not going to return the $100,000 her husband was paid for the locations of his victims' bodies. A senior reporter helped me with my lead:

"Blood money or gift, Joan Olsen isn't giving the $100,000 back." A few months later, that same senior reporter told me what Olsen had done was so obscene that it had to be covered the way they'd covered it. Maybe so, but if that was the kind of story I'd have to write to be a reporter . . .

I never submitted my application for a summer job. Bob and I went to Europe instead, and I realized I didn't know what I was going to do with my life anymore. I just knew that whatever I did wouldn't include asking people how they felt about having their family members die in some horrible manner.

%%

I switched my focus to theatre.

I loved theatre. I was getting great grades in it, and I loved writing plays. While I was interning at the *Province*, the *Ubyssey's* entertainment editor suggested I become a reviewer. I'd get to see plays, for free. I'd learn about theatre. And, best of all, I'd get two tickets to each show, which meant I could bring a date. I'd like to say it was my love of theatre that sold me on the job, but I'd suddenly been handed the only pick-up line I'd ever have that didn't make me feel like an idiot when I used it, because it had the benefit of being true: "I have an extra ticket to a play. Would you like to come with me?"

And since the tickets were free, it wasn't really like a date, unless my date and I ended up making out afterwards—in which case, it was.

I can't remember making out after I went to see the UBC production of *King Lear*, but I must have, because I clearly lost my mind that night. For the first and only time in my reviewing career, I decided to include all the cracks I'd made to my date after the show including, "Martin Schmidt did a brilliant job as Polonius. Unfortunately, he was playing Gloucester." (In case you're not hip to your Shakespeare, Polonius=funny. Gloucester=tragic.)

Martin Schmidt was a professor at UBC. And, as I would soon discover, a beloved one.

The day my review came out, one of my editors had a class with Schmidt. When someone asked him about the show, clearly trying to get his response to the review, he informed the class that my story was right about everyone . . . except him.

My editor was thrilled. My theatre history prof, Dr. Peter Loeffler, wasn't. He called me into his office after class the next day. I knew this wasn't the same scene I'd played with Mr. Murphy. I definitely wasn't failing. Peter had a plummy Swiss accent and spoke English with crisp European precision. "Mah-k," he said, "you're thinking of continuing on in theat-ah, aren't you?"

"Yes," I said. Peter pulled his office door shut, stared at me even more seriously than Mr. Murphy had. "You should," he said. "You really should. You have a passion for it."

I had no clue where this was leading.

"Mah-k, have you ever considered the University of Victoria? They have a *lovely* theat-ah program."

Huh?

"I was in the staff room this afternoon. Everyone was talking about your review," he said. "Very funny. Very clev-ah. Very accurate."

I was too floored by his suggestion of switching schools to respond.

"One of the professors, I can't tell you who . . . " And then he did. "He heard that you were a theatre student. He said he couldn't wait to get you into his class. So he could critique you." Peter told me another professor suggested the same thing. "You can't get a degree without taking classes with both of them. So if you really want to pursue theat-ah—I suggest you do so at another university. I'll miss you," he said. "You're a marvellous student."

"Thank you," I said. Then I got up to leave—although I'm not sure how, because my body was numb. "One more word of advice," he said as I reached for the doorknob. "If you write for the school paper there . . . "

I waited for him to finish.

"Review movies instead."

I transferred to UVic, where I decided to cover my bases by double-majoring in theatre and creative writing.

I didn't write for the *Martlet*, because I wasn't going to be a journalist. When the journalism instructor found out I'd worked at the *Province*, she asked if I'd join the co-op program. She could get me paying work on a newspaper. I passed. I knew I couldn't do it. I'd write plays. Maybe direct. Maybe perform.

I focused my extracurricular time on traditional university pursuits like attending parties and finding a girlfriend. Her name was Barb, and she was in theatre and creative writing too—a year ahead of me. After a few months, we pretty much moved in together. Bob had been right about the sex thing.

In my second year, I enrolled in a class in feature writing because it was taught by Sid Tafler, my favourite writer at Victoria's weekly paper, *Monday Magazine*. Sid was an amazing investigative journalist with an eye for scandals and a talent for scoring career-crushing quotes about politicians. Even if I'd never be a journalist, I knew I'd learn something from him. But I never could have imagined how much. The first night of class, I asked how long he'd been on staff at *Monday*.

"I've never been on staff," he said.

This didn't compute. "But you write there all the time."

"I'm freelance," he said. I'd never heard of "freelance." I'd thought anyone who wrote for a paper worked for that paper and did whatever their editor told them to. Or got fired when they said, "No."

Sid explained freelancing to me. (At the start of the 21st century, half of North America works freelance. In 1984, I think it was just Sid Tafler.)

After class I did something I'd never done before. I asked my teacher if I could buy him a drink. We went to an off-campus pub, where I ordered a pitcher and asked him to tell me more about this mysterious thing called freelancing. Could you really write for anyone? Could you really write anything you wanted to? If there was a story you didn't want to write, could you really say "No"?

My tuition was roughly $1,000 a year. By the time he'd drained the pitcher, I should have written that $1,000 cheque to Sid, who, as I later told Barb, would now and forever after be referred to as "Sid Who Is God."

That summer I freelanced for several small publications. The next year, Sid introduced me to the editor at *Monday*, and I started freelancing for that paper.

And I knew I was going to be a freelancer—or a waiter—when Sheryl offered me the job in Ontario. But now here I was in Williams Lake—working at a real paper, for a real boss, getting in trouble with real police officers. This was definitely not the plan. But it certainly wasn't dull . . .

# Man Shot in Reno, Dies

%%

"The judge wears cowboy boots."

That was the first thing Eric told me about Judge Turner. "When he's wearing his robes, when he's sitting on the bench, he wears cowboy boots."

It was the perfect Cariboo image. Underneath the black silk robes that represent the traditions of queen and country, provincial court judge Quentin Turner wore fancy, hand-tooled, leather cowboy boots. I pictured a John Wayne judge, a hanging judge, a redneck . . .

But when I spotted Judge Turner in the courthouse for the first time he looked more like . . . a dentist. I introduced myself, and he was gracious and friendly. "I'm sure you'll be better than the last reporter," he said.

I smiled. This guy wasn't scary at all.

What was scary was when I walked into the courtroom, settled in to cover my first trial and took out my tape recorder. The sheriff looked at me like I'd exposed myself and told me to put it away.

"But I'm a reporter," I explained.

"And an idiot," he clearly thought as he whispered sharply, "It's illegal to record in a courtroom."

Illegal?

Aside from the feature-writing course with Sid at UVic and the class in high school, I hadn't studied journalism, I'd always just written. And I'd always used a tape recorder to get my quotes right. I definitely wanted to get these quotes right. This was my first trial. And it was big.

The Crown counsel was a heavy hitter. He'd handled some of BC's highest-profile cases. This was supposed to be a straight-forward sexual assault trial, but when Eric heard who was prosecuting, he knew it couldn't be that straightforward. The defendant, Roy Lee Morrel, was charged with sexually assaulting his best friend's four-year-old son. As the Crown laid out the case, I listened, but I didn't look. I was too busy scribbling notes. When we broke for lunch, I told Eric about it. And I told him about the tape recorder thing.

"You didn't know?"

"I forgot," I lied.

"I hope you take good notes," he said. "You know shorthand?"

Shorthand?

"Did Ross know shorthand?"

"Hell no," said Eric. "Ross didn't cover courts. I did."

I ducked into the darkroom, where Kate told me that Eric had misquoted Judge Turner a few weeks before I arrived, and was warned that if it happened again he'd be charged with contempt and tossed in jail. I knew misquoting was bad, but it had never occurred to me that it could land me in prison.

I went back to court and listened to the police officer talk about how he'd caught Morrel. I spent the next five days listening to testimony about what a 40-year-old man had done to a 4-year-old boy. I didn't want to write about the details then, and I don't want to write about them now. The worst part was when the boy came up to testify.

This Norman Rockwell kid practically withered as he sat on his mother's lap and told the judge what his "Uncle Roy" had done to him. "Uncle Roy" watched the boy. And smirked.

On those days I didn't eat lunch. I didn't want to eat at all, and I'm not sure I did. I'd come home, turn on the TV, watch whatever was on—usually cop shows—and try not to think. About anything. People didn't talk about child molesters in the mid-

1980s. The scandals about abusive priests and residential schools hadn't made the news yet. And Olsen . . . No one imagined there was anyone else out there like him. So before that trial, I'd never really thought about the things adults could do to kids.

After the case was over, after Uncle Roy was sentenced to five years in jail, I walked up to the Crown counsel outside the courthouse and asked why he'd flown to the middle of nowhere to prosecute a guy charged with sexually assaulting one kid. He said he could only answer if it was off the record. I've kept it off the record until now. He told me the police believed "Uncle Roy" was responsible for dozens of similar assaults, maybe more than a hundred, but this was the only victim he'd ever attacked who was old enough to testify. I didn't eat at all that day. Or the day after.

%

A couple of nights later, I went with Kate, Abby and Sarah to the bar Tina at the Mohawk station had warned me about. It was every bit as charming as she'd made it sound. Practically everyone there looked like they'd killed somebody, and if they hadn't yet, this was gonna be their lucky night. I saw at least a dozen men and three women who looked like they'd have no problem shooting a man in Reno, or maybe Quesnel, just to watch him die. Two guys tried to pick fights with me in 20 minutes, and I never even left the table. The bouncer eyed me the whole time. Kate told me it was because my leather jacket made me look like a drug dealer—at least by Cariboo standards. She said the last time they were there, Eric got drunk, stood up and announced that everyone in the Cariboo was, "an asshole." I'm not sure how he made it out alive.

We retreated to the safety of the Billy Miner, and I let Sarah drive. I didn't drink often—or much—but that night it seemed like a good idea. Back at the Billy I muttered something about what a creepy way this was to make $1,150 a month. Abby and Kate both stared at me, shocked. They responded in stereo. "That's all they're paying you?"

"Uh, yeah."

Then they laughed. "You gotta be kidding," said Kate. "The student interns all made 12. The *Trib* never pays less than 12—plus car allowance."

Abby agreed. They were certain I was the lowest paid reporter who'd worked for the *Trib* in years. "And you've got more experience than anyone else they ever hired," said Abby. I ordered another drink. And another one after that. I decided I wasn't getting that haircut after all.

A few days later I signed up for a shorthand course, so I wouldn't end up in a cell for a misquote, and I turned down my first weekend assignment. Weekend gigs were a standard part of life at the *Trib*; overtime pay was not. It wasn't quite a six-day week, but everyone in the newsroom assumed they'd spend at least a few hours each weekend covering something.

I'd been drafted into doing stories on my first four weekends. They were all earth-shattering events like a Winnie the Pooh Reading Day at the library. On my fifth weekend the staff decided they wanted to get to know me, so Abby, Kate, Rick and Liz invited me on a hiking trip. I'd never hiked so I was a bit nervous, but the others weren't exactly Olympic athletes, so when they assured me it was a beginner's hike, I was definitely in.

Then Eric announced he wanted me to cover a charity barbecue. I almost said yes, and then I remembered that the worst thing he could do was fire me, and I could go back to having a girlfriend and a life. So I said, "No." I'd heard the word "gobsmacked" before, but I'd never known what it looked like until that moment.

While he was still trying to figure out whether to faint or fire me, I told Eric that I understood my job was covering the news and I would always be ready to cover real news whenever and wherever it happened, but I wouldn't waste my days off showing up at craft fairs and speeches. He stared at me and grunted, then he tried to get Liz to cover the barbecue. I suppose Eric didn't figure it was worth losing me over a few photos of the mayor flipping cheeseburgers.

The good news was that this was my first full weekend off. The bad news was that after the hike, I spent Sunday in bed, in agony. It turned out the leader of the nature hike had his own special definition of "beginners." The lowlight was when I stepped over a fallen tree on the way back down a hill and sprained a muscle in my groin.

I'd always thought the idea of a pulled groin sounded funny—or at least rude—until I pulled mine. Kate walked with me on the way down, making sure I didn't collapse. She suggested that for my next outdoor adventure, I should visit her boyfriend's ranch and learn to ride. Just the thought made me ache even more.

So while I did spend a fair bit of Sunday wishing I'd covered the barbecue instead, that was the last weekend I officially worked for the *Trib*. And as far as the *Trib* was concerned, it turned out to be a dangerous precedent. It wasn't long before Kate, Liz and even Abby stopped working weekends too. Rick had to work weekends, since he covered sports. But since most sports also happened at night, nobody really knew when or if he worked during the week.

But saying no to that barbecue wasn't my most subversive activity. My most subversive activity was lunch. The seeds of rebellion can be as tiny as a single Coney fry.

Eric tried to stop me once. I said I was going for lunch and he asked if I'd done the weather. Yep. What about the police reports? Yep. Forest fire checks? Yep. What about—I'd done that too. And now it was time for a Coney burger and at least three glasses of Coke.

I hung out with Sarah, Abby and Kate after work. I discovered that part of the *Trib* routine was seeing almost everything that played in the two theatres. I even watched my first western. I'd seen them before on TV, but I'd never even thought of watching a western on the big screen.

"Clint," said Kate. "It's classic."

Clint?

I knew Dirty Harry Eastwood. And the Eastwood who monkeyed around with Clive the Gorilla. I didn't know cowboy

Eastwood. But *Pale Rider* was playing, and if I was ever going to see a cowboy movie, this was the place. The theatre was packed and some of the audience members were wearing their stetsons. I'd read *Shane* in grade ten, so I recognized the story of the cowboy who wanders into town and finds redemption. But I didn't know that *Pale Rider* was an Eastwood "greatest hits" package. A mysterious—almost mystical—reluctant gunslinger named Preacher rides into town, takes on the bad guys and wins the hearts of the kid and the girl. A man who doesn't wanna fight, but he's gotta do what he's gotta do. Classic. When Eastwood took down the black hats, everyone in the theatre cheered.

On about my sixth production day, I convinced Rick and Liz to join me for lunch. Eric looked mortified, but if I could do it, there was no reason anyone else could be denied food. It took another week to convince Kate to grab a bite. A week later it was Kate who asked Abby. Abby grumbled about how it was impossible and how this wasn't done and how the world would spin off its axis, but as the rest of us descended the staircase from the editorial office, Abby followed and only Eric remained, staring at his computer, smoking without his cigarette.

As we passed through the back-shop—the place where the ads were assembled and all the words and pictures were arranged to look like a newspaper—one of the women who did layout asked Kate how the "new kid" was working out.

"Great," said Kate. "He makes us take lunch."

# Never Shoot a Stampede Queen

"**W**hat's a Stampede queen?"

Eric showed me the picture in the last *Casual Country*—a half-dozen fresh-faced cowgirls huddled in a bull chute. A bull chute is where they rev up the bulls before the cowboy jumps on them. Then the gate opens and the guy hangs on for dear life and the chance to win a really big belt buckle.

My assignment was to interview this year's crop of women-who-would-be-queens about their lives, ambitions and favourite rodeo events. I was also supposed to take a clever full-colour photo of them somewhere other than a bull chute and get a series of solo headshots.

"Last year we got each of them to write their own stories about different rodeo events and we got a story about how the bull feels when the cowboy rides him. I'd rather not go through that again." Eric actually winced at the memory. Then he pulled out a clipping from a story that had run in the *Trib's* community section a few years earlier. It was written by a past queen.

"At 6:30 p.m. we went to a dinner and dance where we again met the visiting royalty and were introduced to our escorts for the evening. There were about 300 people there and it was a great time until most of the visiting royalty and the chaperones had to leave due to food poisoning."

In the spirit of true community boosterism, the queen concluded, "All in all it was a great weekend, except for the food poisoning." I swear I have not changed a word.

I ran into Kate in the parking lot after work and told her about the assignment. She looked like she'd swallowed a bug. I thought she was mad, that I'd taken one of the big photo ops of the year, so I started to apologize. After she stopped laughing, she wished me luck. "Never," she said—and then she started laughing again— "never shoot a Stampede queen." This was clearly some sort of perverse initiation rite for new reporters.

I first met the princesses in a church basement where they were working on their public speaking. To be fair, there wasn't a Bobby Sue or Linda Lou in the bunch, although it was mandatory for all their names to end with "y" sounds—Sheri, Cindy, Mandy, Christie and Shelley. More realistic career goals included law, dentistry and teaching phys. ed.

They were 17 to 19, pretty in an Ivory Snow ad kinda way— which was a bit distracting for a guy who hadn't seen his girlfriend in almost three months—and as enthusiastic as only beauty contestants can be. These girls had been around rodeos since birth. Many of them started riding about the same time they started walking.

The interviews were pretty bland. Occasionally one of them would express concern about something serious like world hunger or the ethics of abortion, but for the most part I got the feeling those were things they'd seen Miss America worrying about on TV. But becoming a Stampede queen wasn't just a chance to wear a pretty dress in a parade, it was "a dream," and everyone I interviewed said so.

"I've always dreamed of being a Stampede queen," 17-year-old Mandy informed me with terrifying sincerity. Her other goals included becoming an actress, secretary, model, stewardess or all of the above. The other would-be queens had similar stories. They'd all wanted to be queen since they were little girls reading stories about princesses.

Trying to take their photos was about as easy as posing cats. I'm sure an ace photographer would have thought it was a breeze, but cheesecake shots were a new experience for me. The girls all wanted to look their best and were perpetually disappearing to adjust their hair, their makeup, their cleavage or whatever it is princesses fix when they're getting their pictures taken.

I showed up for an outdoor photo and it rained. I showed up for an indoor photo, and Christie had her hair mussed from riding and refused to let me remove my lens cap.

Finally I managed a series of pictures with them sitting on a fence—very Huck Finn—and another set with them in a horse trailer. I whipped off the profiles and waited for the call from *Playboy* telling me I'd been discovered and they were flying me to the mansion to write Playmate bios.

Sheri's interests include basketball, jazz dancing, riding and skiing. Mandy coaches gymnastics and enjoys working with small children. Christie likes acting, camping, canoeing and making new friends. Yes, really.

The next night Eric and Andrea took me to the high school gym to check out a folksinger, Geoff Patenaude. He only played a few songs, but they were catchy. My favourite was, "A Horsefly road is rough, but a Chevy truck is tough." The image of a horse-fly road cracked me up.

"You should do a story on him," said Eric.

Eric invited Geoff to our table. I asked if we could talk sometime and he invited me for dinner on Sunday.

"Sure," I said. "Where do you live?"

He looked at me like I was an idiot. How could I not know where he lived?

"Horsefly."

I looked to Eric and Andrea to see if they were laughing. They weren't. Did this mean the horsefly road was actually . . . the road to a place called Horsefly?

Geoff scrawled directions on a napkin.

Apparently I was dining in Horsefly. I had a hunch how it might have earned its name, so I made sure I brought some bug spray. I'd been bitten by a horsefly once—and until then I'd never imagined a bug could actually take a chunk out of your skin.

I drove the Horsefly road with Geoff's song playing in my head as my Toyota spewed gravel and dirt from behind the rear tires.

Geoff had the type of idyllic country home that seduces city folk into thinking rural life is all sunsets and clear skies with nary a ruptured septic tank to be seen. And I had a perfect meal—exactly what you'd expect from a horse logger in Horsefly—vegetarian lasagna. "We don't eat meat," he said. "I hope that's okay." A Cariboo vegetarian? Maybe that was the news story? We ate in the living room with his wife and kids, and then watched Bugs Bunny until there was no excuse for not getting on with the interview.

Geoff and his wife invited me back, but I never took them up on it. My city-boy reserve was unequipped to deal with that kind of casual country hospitality.

# *Casual Country*

///

A newspaper supplement is normally made up of about two dozen pages loaded with ads, surrounded by a bit of brief, boosterish copy disguised as "consumer reporting." *Casual Country* was a 150-page magazine about everything and everybody in the Cariboo. "Looks great," I said, as Eric proudly flipped through the 1984 edition.

"Glad you like it, you'll be writing this one." He was exaggerating, but it didn't feel like it. He wanted features on all the mills, several regional artists and all the rodeo events.

My first big story was about a prize-winning roper. His ranch was just outside town. Jim Munson was a wiry cowboy the same age as me. When I told him I'd never seen a rodeo, Jim took me into his living room and popped a tape in the VCR so we could watch his heroes and he could explain his sport and the skill involved.

Then he took me to the yard and let me watch as he hopped on his chestnut-coloured horse, Brandy, and held a lasso like he was living in a cowboy movie. "There's dozens of variables in calf roping," he said. "That's why I love it. Never know where the calf's gonna go."

He hopped off Brandy and asked if I wanted to ride. It wasn't really a question. "C'mon," he said. I tried to think of the last time I'd been on a horse. I was sure I'd been on a horse before. Then I realized—not a horse, but a pony. And I think some nice old man had held my hand for the entire ride so I wouldn't fall.

I stared at Brandy, praying she wouldn't attack.

"You'll be fine," said Jim as he boosted me onto the um, horse seat. I slid my feet into the stirrups as he held Brandy still.

"How much is a horse like this worth?" I asked.

"I paid $10,000 for Brandy," he said. "And she's worth a lot more now that she's trained."

I was on a $10,000 horse. As Brandy stepped onto some rocks, I was sure I was going to break her. Jim told me how to steer, but I was determined not to piss Brandy off, so I let the horse take me wherever she wanted to go. It was the perfect metaphor for my life in Williams Lake and I didn't even realize it.

The next day Eric handed me another map to another place I'd never heard of. And a picture of a very short totem pole.

"The artist was just commissioned to do a piece for the Friendship Centre," he said.

The, uh, what?

"It's like a community centre for the Natives. I told him you could meet him Friday."

And that was all I knew about Wilbur Marshall—that and the fact that he lived more than an hour out of town, at a place accessible only by roads that looked like gravel pits with weeds. Driving there I had to stop twice—for cows. I'd never stopped for cows before. They didn't seem to care much about Toyotas.

As I waited for the second herd of cattle to clear the road, it occurred to me that I'd never spoken to a Native person before. I vaguely remembered visiting a reserve once with my mom and seeing traditional ceremonies reenacted, but I wasn't sure if it was a genuine childhood memory or something I'd seen on TV. Or maybe it was a luau in Honolulu, when I was a kid?

The reserve didn't look anything like I'd expected. The houses were modern suburban boxes, the kind of assembly-line places developers refer to as "housing units." There were a few attractive, modern buildings—the store, the town hall—but most of the houses looked abandoned. People lived in them, but they sure didn't seem to like them.

Some yards were filled with abandoned bikes, trikes, sleds, bats, balls, hoops, Frisbees and broken toys. Other units had burnt-out cars, leftover engines and pieces of scrap metal on their yellowing lawns. I'm sure there were some well-kept homes, but it was the unloved "units" that stuck out for me that day.

Wilbur's yard was tidy, and his place looked a bit more like a home than the others. When Wilbur's door opened, I wasn't sure what to expect. I didn't even have a stereotype in my head to work with. So the soft timbre of his voice, the musicality of his speech, that was something new to me. His hushed tones were nearly drowned by the hum of the fan in the cool basement workshop where we spoke, but there was something about his voice that hypnotized me. I scrawled down that he spoke like "a man who has been to the depths of his soul and come back to tell about it." (Hey, I was 22.)

He'd been to jail. He wouldn't tell me what for. And since the story was about his art, not a run for Parliament, I didn't push that hard.

"It was alcohol that landed me in jail."

"For what?" I asked again.

"I don't put the blame on me. I don't put the blame on anyone who goes to prison. It's their weaknesses that put them there. Mine happened to be alcohol."

Marshall had lived in Vancouver, but after he got out of jail he moved back to the reserve because alcohol wasn't allowed there. He figured it would help him stay sober. The reserve was famous for its dry policy, and that summer, a documentary crew flew in to profile it as a national success story.

Marshall had just turned 37, and he said his carving was "a search for who I am." I asked if he had any pictures of the work he'd done—and sold—so I could use them in the story. He shook his head, smiled, laughed. "I never really got into carving to make a big thing out of it or anything like that, eh. It's just my life."

"I'd always been interested in carving, but it was in prison I finally learned the art. I'd never had any patience before. Outside I was always high strung . . . always on the go-go-go."

I had trouble picturing him on the go-go-go.

"I'd run into all of these . . . problems."

The problems I could picture, even through the smiles.

He walked me through his workshop, showing me his mini-totems, plaques and pictures made from yellow cedar. The art I saw was haunting in pretty much the way I found Wilbur Marshall haunting. He'd found something in prison, but I couldn't shake the feeling that he'd lost a lot more before he got there.

I asked how much money he made as a carver.

He laughed again. "I don't take money," he said.

"But your commission—"

"People ask me to do things and I do them. I carve for friends, family. I carve so I can tell the stories inside me."

He showed me a picture he'd kept of the wall hanging he'd made for the Friendship Centre. It showed the sun, a raven and an eagle lined up beside each other.

"I wanted to put them on the same level," he said. "Not like a regular totem, one on top of the other. Not one more powerful than the other, not one less powerful than the other, not one at the bottom . . . because," and he paused again, "there's a lot of problems today."

"So how do you choose your images?"

"Ravens, they're strong. And I like black . . . People say black, it's a very dark colour, and the dark side. But why? You look at it and it's beautiful, it's—" And he paused again. "Does it have to be white to be beautiful?"

I stared at the picture of his raven.

"I like carving animals because it's a way to get close to the people that made them," Staring at the ceiling, his mind drifting far away, he asked—not me, but the air I suppose—"How could He do this? How could He make something as beautiful as this?"

On the road back to Williams Lake I ran into another herd of cattle. This time the cows parted to reveal a bull, and it stood there staring at my car. I was afraid to honk. There are some things they don't teach you when you get your licence in the city. I can parallel park like a wizard, and I'm great at signalling my turns, but I couldn't remember anything on the driver's test about meeting a bull. So I waited. And waited. I wasn't sure if the bull would consider honking a threat, so I just stared at it, and it stared blankly back at me, and then, deciding that my Toyota wasn't worth a challenge, it ambled on.

# *Tourist Trapped*

I still **don't know** what prompted him to call me—or maybe the better question is "who?"—but Mitch Kiley wanted me to meet him.

Mitch Kiley is the type of character Paul St. Pierre wrote about—an old-time Cariboo charmer. There were roads named after his family. So when he called and said he wanted me to drop by his jewellery shop so he could show me his new bear trap, I was thrilled. It was an "in" with the community and a terrific excuse to leave the office.

I walked down Oliver and asked the clerk where I could find Kiley. She pointed to the back room.

He didn't bellow a "Howdy," but he was the type of guy who could have. He looked to be a robust 50—although he was probably at least 10 years older than that. After a hearty handshake, I asked where his bear trap was. He gave me a proud smile and pointed to the table in the middle of the room. All I saw was a large metal ring with an arrow-shaped prong. If I'd had to guess, I would have figured it was the sign for a giant airport's men's room.

"Where is it?" I asked again.

He pointed to the men's room sign again. "There she is."

"That's the bear trap?"

"Yup."

I knew he was a local pioneer—probably even an advertiser—so I had to be polite.

"You gotta be kidding."

And with a wounded tone that made me ashamed of my rudeness, he answered, "Nope. That's my bear trap."

I took my clipboard out of my camera bag. "So how does it work?" It didn't look like a bear trap to me, but the only live bears I'd ever seen were in cages, so what did I know. This guy had probably seen bears frolicking in the woods, eating honey and stealing picnic baskets with Boo Boo.

"It's a very tricky bear trap," explained Mitch. "What you need is a handful of fresh berries, the hoop, an axe and a lot of courage."

As he talked, I scrawled everything onto the yellow paper in my clipboard. "The hunter goes into the woods and stalks the bear. Once he gets close enough, the hunter starts tossing the berries over the bear's head. Preferably strawberries," he said and then paused to make sure I was getting this down. "When the bear bends down to pick up the berries, the hunter races towards it and sticks the arrow up the bear's rectum."

I looked up from my notes—eyes wide. Up the bear's what? I was too stunned to laugh. Almost too stunned to talk.

"His ass," said Mitch, like I was too thick to understand the word "rectum."

"And then?" I asked.

"And then," says Mitch, as dryly as if he were reading the instruction manual for his new Winchester, "you flip the ring over the nearest tree stump and he's trapped. You do it fast though, 'cause by this time the bear's pretty damn angry."

"I can imagine," I said, trying to do just that. My brain was still trying to process . . . You stick the prong where? And that's when I started to laugh like a guy who just heard about a mob of angry cookie elves. Mitch stood there, arms folded, looking very serious indeed.

He didn't seem crazy, so he had to be kidding, right? I stopped laughing and decided to play along.

"Wouldn't this be an awfully dangerous way to trap a bear?"

"Very dangerous," said Mitch.

"So who else uses this trap besides you?"

He listed off the names of four other pillars of the community who had roads named after them.

"Really?" I was getting nervous. Maybe people here were crazy enough to stick a prong up a bear's butt.

"That's right," said Mitch. "It may be dangerous, but there's no real sport in hunting bears with a gun. It's the same as shooting hogs in a barrel. But you get a grizzly with one of these, and it's probably the greatest accomplishment a hunter can achieve."

"I guess it is," I said soberly. I stared down at my notepad. Maybe if I kept looking at my notes, I wouldn't laugh. Then I asked his advice for hunters who'd like to try his trap themselves.

"Don't panic." His expression was still dead serious.

Then it hit me. "But, um, what if there's no stump?"

"If there's no stump, that's where you need the axe, 'cause you better make one pretty darn fast." He told me the trap had existed for generations, but his version was unique because it had a bigger prong. "So you can hunt grizzlies."

When I asked what kind of hunters would most likely use this method, Mitch summed it up in one word: "Drunk."

Okay, I could play too. "So have you patented it?" I asked.

"Not yet," he said. "Haven't got around to it."

"Have you caught a bear with it yet?"

"Haven't actually used it myself. But I seen some fellows that have. Even attended a few of their funerals. They just didn't cut those stumps quick enough."

I was sure Mitch was kidding. Okay, I was pretty sure. But with my reputation I wasn't taking any chances.

I walked back to the office, trying to figure out how or whether to write this up.

"That's Mitch Kiley," said Abby. "Why would he make up a story? It must be true."

Kate told me I had to write the story, because Mitch was a major advertiser. "Even if he is making it up, what's going to happen to you if you accuse him of making it up?"

Just as I was bracing to write about Kiley's bold new invention, Stan came upstairs. Abby told Stan about my scoop. He kept a straight face for a few seconds before he started to howl. "Oh

God," said Stan laughing like he'd just heard about the cookie strikers. "The old hoop trap? You didn't fall for it, did you?"

Abby and Kate grinned at me like, just maybe, they were in on it too. And I sat there turning the colour of a strawberry and looking, well, em-bear-assed.

"So what are you going to do with the story?" Kate asked. "After all, the trap doesn't work."

"Sure it does," I said. And I wrote a story explaining seriously and in precise detail everything Mitch Kiley had told me about his wonderful invention. I even phoned the environmental protection officer for a quote and got him to confirm that the arrow-hoop trap is not a safe, government-approved method for hunting bears.

"But," my story concluded, "it's extremely effective at catching gullible tourists."

# Enviro-Metalists
# Tell All

///

After a few months in town, I'd realized the only people besides Stan who were thrown by the long hair were the loggers, because they thought I was a hippie. As far as I could tell they weren't opposed to the concept of free love, at least as long as it was free after a few drinks. And nobody seemed to mind the nearby cannabis-growing communes either. This was, after all, the wild west coast. It was that legendary Vancouver environmentalism that made locals want to take a chainsaw to any longhairs from "the coast."

I was visiting a mill for *Casual Country*, learning the ins and outs of sorters, stackers, cutters and "optimizing edger scanners" when my guide steered me through the lunchroom to get to the next high-tech, wood-slashing gizmo.

I was wearing my standard uniform, jeans and a sweatshirt. My hair was a little past shoulder-length and my beard was in desperate need of a trim, and when we hit the lunchroom, one of the good ol' boys, pot-bellied, late 40s, looked up, spotted me and said, "Ain't she cute."

The other two good ol' boys in the room chuckled.

"She's yer typa girl ain't she, Joe?"

Joe looked up, sussing whether he had to slug me to defend his manhood. "Naaah," said Joe, "I think Charlie'd like her."

Charlie, who looked like he used trees for toothpicks, scowled, and the final scene from *Easy Rider* flashed before my eyes.

My guide, a city slicker like myself, mumbled something about new machines and pulled me out the door towards some spinning metal things that were chewing up logs like a family of beavers from hell.

So I was a little wary a few days later when Eric sent me out of town to ask Tom Adams to show me his new machine.

Tom was a longtime "feller." "Feller," or "faller," is a proper but much less cool word for "lumberjack." That means he was a lumberjack until, I guess, *Monty Python*'s "Lumberjack Song" convinced everyone to adopt the word "feller." So tree cutters were fellers just like "harvesting" was the preferred, um, buzz-word for "cutting trees." Tom was mid-40s, wiry and looked like he could dead-lift a tree out of the ground the way most people pull weeds. He wore a hard hat, which also didn't go with the lumberjack image, but probably made the insurance companies happy.

Before I could interview him, though, Tom wanted to inter-view me. He was looking at my hair. "You're not one of those enviro-metalists, are you?"

The honest answer was "Yes," but the honest answer would have meant I'd driven an hour to the edge of nowhere only to turn around without a story or a photo, so that Eric could order me to drive back to apologize and do the interview.

"Not really," I said.

Tom nodded, grunted. "Good. Damn enviro-metalists are ruining this business. Do you know how many of my friends have been laid off because of those idiots?"

I grunted too, asked what he wanted to show me, and he waved his callused hand to present a machine that looked like a life-sized version of something a sci-fi crazed kid would make with a Lego set. Who else but a 10-year-old boy would think of building something with tractor rollers, pincers and a buzz saw? Give the thing an evil grin and a plan to rule the world—or at least rob a bank or two—and it looked like it should be fighting Green Lantern.

"It's a danglehead processor," said Tom. "It's pretty much a mill on wheels." And he patted the machine like a horse. "This baby will chop a tree, buck it, limb it, cut it to length and stack it. And you just need one person to run it. Do you know how many men it used to take to do this? How many days? 'Mazing," said Tom.

Then Tom took me over to the stack of lumber he'd made that day with his cool new toy. The thing could even haul the trees, I mean timber or lumber or wood . . . to the landing. Tom told me how much it cost, how well it worked and, of course, how much he cared about the forest. "I love trees," he said.

When I wrote the story, I had to talk about the incredible technological breakthrough and how this processor could do the processing of a half-dozen full-time loggers and what a great thing that was for the mills. Fortunately, I didn't have to say the reason they were laying so many people off was because of those damn enviro-metalists.

%

Tom was right, though. I was a west-coast kid with a university education from the city where Greenpeace was born, and that meant being an enviro-metalist and wanting to save whales and hug trees was pretty much my birthright.

That's why I was so excited to meet the friendly people at Ducks Unlimited. I couldn't believe there were actually people in Williams Lake who devoted their time to saving wetlands to preserve animals.

I was even more surprised to find out what a huge organization this was. When I got to the office, I expected graffiti or broken windows, but the place was spotless. Maybe this town was more liberal than I thought.

Randy Harkin was one of the movers and shakers I'd met at that Kiwanis lunch. He was either a dentist or a pharmacist, and he was also an environmentalist. I know this because he told me. "I'm an environmentalist," he said. "That's what we're all about here—preserving the environment, preserving the wetlands."

Randy told me how much money they'd raised, how many members they had locally and worldwide and how much wetland they'd saved for ducks.

If I wasn't a reporter I would have joined on the spot—but I figured signing a membership card would be a conflict of interest. I drove back to the office, wrote the story, filed it and, a few minutes later, Eric called me over to his office.

"I'm surprised you liked these guys," he said.

Surprised? Even their name was great. Ducks Unlimited—who could argue with that?

"They're saving the environment," I said. "In a place like this, I think that's pretty cool."

Eric smiled and this time it looked like that smile was moments away from a laugh. "And do you know what they do with the ducks they save?"

Sure I did. "Look at them with binoculars. Catalogue them. Take pictures."

"Shoot them," said Eric.

This didn't compute. "With guns?"

"They're hunters."

My jaw dropped like it was on a cartoon hinge. I stared at the story on Eric's computer screen. Eric laughed.

"Mind if I revise that a bit?"

After Eric stopped laughing, he nodded. "Thought you might want to."

%

A few days after learning about saving wetland for shooting ducks, I went to interview a trapper to find out how animals are turned into coats and shoes.

Jess Ketchum was a big bubba in jeans, a flannel lumberjack shirt and a ball cap with a trucking logo on it. "I love animals," he said as we wandered towards his trapline. "I'm an environmentalist," he said. Obviously this word had a very different definition in the Cariboo. Most of the proud environmentalists

I knew back at UVic wouldn't eat lunch with me because I ate burgers that weren't made from wheat berries.

"I have to live off the land and that means making sure the animal population is well managed. You can't take too many animals one year or you won't eat the next year. Understand?"

I nodded that I did.

"I got two beaver colonies out here," he continued, as he gestured at his domain. "And if you don't catch enough beaver each year, they'll eat the whole food supply. Starve themselves. Catch too many, no beavers next year." This was very Canadian. I knew our country started as a beaver brokerage, and that if not for the brief craze for beaver-pelt hats back in olde England, America would have been a whole lot bigger.

Jess told me to get on the back of his all-terrain vehicle, which is a cool name for a big, goofy motorized tricycle. As we zipped along, it seemed like he was going out of his way to ride over hills and under low-hanging branches to see if I'd fall off. It took an hour before I realized that was exactly what he was doing.

Jess didn't kill animals, he "harvested" them—the same way the loggers "harvested" trees. He'd been keeping his family fed by harvesting thousands of small woodland creatures in a 250-square-mile stretch of woods near Horsefly for nearly 20 years. That year he'd set 400 traps, and, according to his logs, had caught 100 beaver, 100 red squirrel, 500 muskrat, 30 mink, 30 marten, a dozen coyote, a few otter, ermine and fox—and one lynx, which sounds more like a Scrabble word than an animal. Luckily for me, he hadn't harvested anything that day, so the only pictures I managed to get were of Jess inspecting his nasty-looking empty traps and Jess on his funky tricycle, beaming at the camera.

I forgot to ask if he was a member of Ducks Unlimited.

# A Typical Cariboo Killing

///

Every defendant gets at least three names. I assume the theory is that it makes cases of mistaken identity less likely. The reality is that it makes criminals sound more dramatic.

Andrew Arthur Milton was a 21-year-old Native on trial for manslaughter for one of the higher-profile crimes in recent Cariboo history. At about 8:30 on a Friday night in the summer of 1983, three people were stabbed in front of Williams Lake's only liquor store. One woman, Pearl Ritchie, a 56-year-old with "no fixed address," died that night. There were obviously dozens of witnesses—it was still light out when it happened—but nobody saw the killer well enough to identify him. Nobody ever saw much when the victims were "Troopers."

I was never able to determine exactly where the name came from—even the old-timers and history buffs had forgotten—but "Trooper" was Williams Lake slang for "homeless drunk," and most Troopers were Native. The best theory I heard about the name was that it was a holdover from a social work outfit that had tried to organize the homeless people, and the name had been designed to give them a sense of community spirit. It stuck, but it didn't seem to empower anyone. The *Trib* staff even played baseball against some Troopers once, in a game set up by an enthusiastic young social worker. As bad as the *Trib* staffers were, it was a little like the New York Yankees taking on the outpatients from *One Flew Over the Cuckoo's Nest*.

I didn't know the history of the manslaughter case, but Staff Sergeant O'Donnell wanted me to know it was one of the biggest investigations his detachment had ever conducted. He said they'd always been fairly sure "who dunnit," but this was one case where the Mounties couldn't get their man. When they checked the hotels, the reserves, the ranches, no one knew anything. No one had seen Andrew Arthur Milton.

A few months before I arrived in town, Pearl Ritchie's son, James, had written a letter to the *Trib* that could be summed up by his final line: "If the victims had been White, the murderer would already be in jail."

The police weren't sure how to respond without looking like they were attacking the victim's son. The fact that Staff Sergeant O'Donnell was talking to me like we were pals made it clear how much the criticism stung. "We knew who did it. Everybody knew who did it. But what can we do if no one will tell us where he is?"

It stung even more that Milton evaded them for over two years. I asked Eric about the letter and whether he thought it was fair.

"Why do you think I printed it?" he said. He didn't have to smile to get across his suspicions. Maybe Milton was hard to find, but was finding him really a top priority?

The RCMP finally caught Milton after he broke into a gas station in Prince George to steal some smokes. This time the victim was a White man with an alarm system.

When the police brought Milton back to Williams Lake, they were thrilled to finally tell their story—to let the community, especially the Native community, know the murder had not been forgotten. It's just that the police, like Pearl Ritchie's family, would probably have felt better if their criminal had seemed, well, a bit more criminal. O'Donnell told me that after the three-hour interrogation was over, after a complete confession was made, Andrew Arthur Milton looked at the officers, cried and said, "Thank you."

The day before Milton's case came to court, I'd covered the

trial of a pair of thugs who'd held up an elderly couple at rifle point. They had criminal records that stretched to Horsefly. My favourite item on one of their rap sheets: stealing a rifle from a police cruiser. Both of them grinned as Judge Turner sentenced them each to seven years. You could see them calculating exactly how much time they'd really serve and who they'd get even with when they got out. They were evil bastards, and all jail was going to do was give them time to build up their already impressive muscles in the gym. When Crown counsel Kevin Holland described the elderly couple they'd tied up and left to die and the two men laughed, I found myself reconsidering my opposition to the death penalty. These two weren't even killers, as far as the police knew, but I had no trouble believing the world would be better off without them.

Andrew Arthur Milton had a criminal record too. He got drunk, stole things, sold them and got drunk again. He'd never hurt anyone, hardly looked like he could. He was a small guy with a sweet face. He looked more like the type of guy people charged with manslaughter beat up for kicks.

But that summer night in 1983, when he was 18, Andrew went to a party and got really stoned. Somebody insulted him, and he pulled a knife.

A friend who served some time in prison once told me, "It's the small guys you gotta watch out for in a fight. A big guy will just hit you. If a small guy jumps you, that means he's carrying."

Carrying?

My friend translated: "A weapon. Or he's crazy. A big guy might hurt you. But if a small guy gets you down, the small guy will kill you."

Andrew's brother tried to calm things down before somebody else pulled a weapon—or took Andrew's knife away and stabbed him with it. He didn't want Andrew to get in trouble, didn't want him to get hurt. So he told his brother to get out and cool off. Andrew left to start his own party. Outside the liquor store, three Troopers were looking for money.

There were always Troopers outside the liquor store looking

for money. A witness said one of the Troopers asked Andrew to buy him a drink. Instead of ignoring him, or tossing him a quarter, Andrew stabbed him. Then he went after the two others—a man and a woman, Pearl. The same witness said that a few seconds later it was like "the woman jumped sideways."

Andrew's lawyer told the police his client thought the Troopers were threatening him. "Andrew thought he was being mugged and that's why he pulled his knife." The idea of three old drunks mugging an 18-year-old didn't strike anyone as all that plausible a motive for murder.

What nobody disagreed on was what happened next. Andrew swung fast and wild, stabbing the two men and then the woman. He stabbed Pearl Ritchie five times, three in the heart.

Then Andrew ran. He went to the hotel he was living in and threw out his flannel shirt because it was covered with blood. He threw his knife in a trash bin. Then he started running again.

The police suspected he'd hidden at a few reserves, but after they finally found him, they weren't all that interested in where he'd been hiding or who had kept him hidden. Andrew admitted it was a few months before he skipped town. He ran, but he didn't run far. He stayed in the interior of BC—never straying further than Alberta. He pulled a few B and Es, but he'd never hurt anyone. For two years he and his girlfriend lived in a series of motel rooms and abandoned cabins, and night after night Andrew would wake up in a cold sweat after having the same nightmare—"nightmares of blood on the ground."

Andrew told the court he didn't remember the stabbings. But as Holland described the crime for the judge, Andrew nodded. And when Holland asked if this was accurate, Andrew nodded again. He remembered throwing away the knife—but he couldn't remember the stabbings. He remembered the blood on his shirt—but he couldn't remember whose blood it was. Andrew Arthur Milton sat in the docket and pleaded guilty to a crime he didn't remember, but knew beyond any reasonable doubt that he'd committed.

Friends of the victims watched from the public gallery,

knowing this man had killed Pearl Ritchie, but was not a killer. The Crown and the public defender both asked for the same term—five to seven years. They knew Andrew had murdered a woman and stabbed two men. They knew he had to go to jail. But no one looked happy about it. Before passing the sentence, Judge Turner told the court what the police were dying to: "Some people probably think the police just chuck their old cases in a basket and forget about them, but that is not the case."

Then Judge Turner pronounced a sentence of five years, sounding almost ashamed of what he had to do. He called the murder "a typical Cariboo killing," which he described as "a drunken event usually involving a knife."

Judge Turner wished Andrew well in jail and decreed that psychiatric help should be found for the typical Cariboo killer. Maybe, in a prison bunk, the nightmares of blood on the ground would finally go away. And when the sentence was handed down, Andrew nodded at the judge and said in a voice that was nearly a whisper, "Thank you."

# *Designated Driver*

///

A few days later I covered what I guess you could call a typical Cariboo car accident.

I've never had much sympathy for drunk drivers—never had any sympathy for them, really. Six days after I got my licence, I took my brother for a drive to show off my new-found mobility. We were right out front of the Hotel Vancouver when a drunk driver connected with my dad's Honda Civic. If we hadn't been wearing seatbelts, we would have spent the entire night at St. Paul's Hospital while doctors picked pieces of the windshield from our faces. The front of dad's car was crushed like an eggshell. My brother, who rarely shut up, was pale and dead quiet. Years later, when I learned the term, I realized he'd been in shock.

I was so scared that I never wanted to get behind the wheel of a car again. Ever since then, I'd been appalled that being drunk helps killers get reduced sentences. If anything, I'd toss all drunk drivers in jail for attempted murder, since I figure driving drunk is pretty much the vehicular version of Russian roulette.

So I was not particularly interested in attending the sentencing hearing for Denny Bryan James, a drunk driver charged with manslaughter. Then I listened to Judge Turner as he sat on the bench and recapped the story.

The 22-year-old unemployed mill worker and his best friend, Mike, and their best girls had gone to a party. They were all in their early 20s. They'd all gotten drunk and maybe a little stoned. One of the girls suggested they go for a ride in Mike's pickup.

Denny didn't think it was a good idea. Everybody was drunk, they were having fun, why not stay at the party? But the girls wanted to go for a ride, have a party of their own. Denny'd had less to drink than Mike, so he agreed to drive—as long as they stayed in the countryside, where there weren't any other cars, where no one could get hurt. At 22, when two girls want to party with you and your best friend, how many guys would say no?

Everybody piled in. The girls got in the back, giggling and laughing. Denny and Mike got in the front. They were gonna find a spot in the woods. They had a case of beer, a couple of blankets and two drunk, giggling girlfriends. They were gonna have a real good time.

Denny stuck to the back roads. He didn't want to run into the police or anybody else. He was being careful. After all, he knew he was drunk. They came to a hill and everyone wanted to drive up. That's where they'd party.

Denny was worried about the hill. It was pretty steep. And it had rained the day before. It was pretty muddy. Mike said his truck could handle the climb. Denny got about halfway up the hill before his wheels started spewing mud. There was no traction. "It's not safe," said Denny. And even though everyone was prodding him to keep going, Denny decided to back up. He was being careful.

Even the Crown counsel agreed that what happened next was a freak accident that could have happened to anyone, drunk or sober. It's just that a sober person probably wouldn't have gone up that hill on that night. One of the front tires tucked itself into a muddy pothole, and when Denny put the pickup in reverse, the tire jammed. Mike was leaning out the window to see what was happening when his truck tipped on its side and crushed him.

Judge Turner went easy on Denny Bryan James. He was sentenced to a year's probation and some community service. No one, not even Mike's family, wanted Denny in jail. Everybody in the courtroom—the judge, the Crown counsel, even the sheriffs—looked uncomfortable.

Most times when you say, "It could have happened to anyone," what you're really thinking is, "What a moron." But when I sat in the press box watching Denny James walk away with the sheriffs, it was impossible not to think, "It could have happened to me."

# Stampede Queens
# Dethroned

%%

One of the perks of working as a reporter in the boonies is that you can occasionally resell your best stories to the big-city dailies. Not only do you get a bit of extra money, but the dream is that one day even the most cynical editors at the big papers will be so dazzled by your sparkling prose, so overwhelmed by your initiative, that they will rescue you from your tiny newspaper with offers of fame and fortune in the big city. At least I'm pretty sure it's just a dream, since it's probably just as likely a casting agent will spot you eating Coney fries at the Dog 'n' Suds and say, "Kid, I'm gonna make you a star."

Eric explained "stringing" to me when I covered Milton's manslaughter trial. I sold it to the *Vancouver Sun*, and I must have done a decent job, because the editor offered me an assignment.

The *Province* had run a lot of stories about Judge Turner. (This was not quite the same paper I'd worked for. They'd become a tabloid—and dumped "Vancouver" from their name to sell more issues in the burbs—so all their stories were short, bright and breezy, or sensational and kinda sleazy.) Before I arrived in Williams Lake, there had been a series of cases bungled by the BC Ministry of Human Resources—the ministry responsible for child welfare—that had ended up in court, and the *Province* sent a reporter to cover them. The reporter wrote a series of stories with headlines on the theme of "Judge Blasts MHR." Eric showed me the other stories.

In the first MHR-blasting case, a social worker somehow managed to lose the file of a girl who had run away from her parents 15 times. When she ran away again, the ministry returned her again. The lost file explained that she'd run away because her father was sexually abusing her. Judge Turner called the ministry official who had lost the file "irresponsible and absurdly stupid." After sending a girl back to an abusive home, I thought the caseworker was lucky they weren't calling him "defendant."

In other cases, the MHR seemed to be using the old playbook from the days when the federal government removed Native kids from their homes and placed them in residential schools, except this time the panacea was foster care. "Turner's fighting to stop them from pulling Native kids out of their homes," Eric said. "Trying to at least make sure they get placed with other Natives. It's a great story."

The editor at the *Sun* heard there was another "Judge Blasts MHR" story on the way, and he was tired of being scooped, so he wanted me on it. Bonus money. A byline in the *Sun*. I was thrilled.

There was only one problem. The judge didn't blast MHR. During the lunch break, the teenager's lawyer filled me in on the details. Her client left an abusive home, ran away and fell into petty crime to support himself on the streets. She knew he could go to adult prison, but she believed he still had a chance to turn his life around if he went to a juvenile facility that had counsellors as well as guards. So far the MHR caseworker had been helpful, and the lawyer planned to bend over backwards to stay in the ministry's good books. Judge Turner was critical of the ministry's handling of the boy's file, but tactful. It was still a good story, but it wasn't the story the *Sun* had expected, and I wouldn't have been surprised if the editor killed my file. Since the *Sun* arrived in the Cariboo a day late, I phoned Barb to find out about my story. Did it make it in? How much did they edit? Did they spell my name right?

It was a banner headline on page three. No byline. I was renamed "Special to the *Sun*." But I was still excited, until Barb read me the lead. "A judge and a defence lawyer joined forces Monday to accuse the Human Resources Ministry of ignoring the problems of a juvenile offender." Every other line remained pretty much intact, every comma as I'd dictated it. All the editor had done was written a new lead that made the story completely inaccurate.

I called the lawyer and Judge Turner, explained what happened and offered to send them copies of the story I'd actually filed. The lawyer screamed at me. She told me I might cost her kid that placement, get him thrown in adult prison, ruin his life. Judge Turner was angry too, but just muttered, "Typical."

It was several weeks before I finally got the cheque from the *Sun* for my big story. Thirty bucks. Addressed to Neil Leisen-Young at the *Williams Cake Tribune*. Fame and fortune.

※

My next big brush with fame—or at least infamy—was when I discovered the Stampede queens had declared me public enemy number one. I was at my desk and could hear someone screaming from downstairs that they weren't leaving until they found "that horrible Mark Leiner-Young."

As I approached the stairs I heard the screamer repeating the words, "How dare he call himself a photographer?" To be honest I would never dare call myself a photographer, at least nowhere within earshot of anybody who'd seen me try to load a camera.

When I got to our receptionist's desk, the banshee was waving a copy of *Casual Country* in one hand and trying to poke holes in the pictures of the princesses with the index finger of her other. "Look at this," she shrieked, flailing away with that lethal finger. "These girls are in tears. They want to kill themselves!"

She stopped shrieking just long enough to tell me she was Christie's aunt. I looked at the pictures for the first time and I could see why some of the girls might be a tad—okay, maybe a pretty huge tad—upset. Two girls looked fine, but Christie was overexposed and had this seriously stoned look like the '60s hadn't been good to her at all. Cindy was all braces, her eyes glazed and her blonde hair obliterated by the black background. And Sheri, easily the prettiest of the five, had a horsey smile I certainly hadn't noticed when I was lusting after her. Her blonde Farrah Fawcett locks were cropped by the frame to the point where she looked like that girl who ballooned into a blueberry in *Charlie and the Chocolate Factory.*

"How dare you call yourself a photographer?" the banshee screeched again. She informed me that more friends and relatives were going to come after me—a posse of angry aunties. And this was the Cariboo. They'd probably have guns.

I didn't know what to say. They were terrible pictures. So I used the time-honoured cop-out reporters have relied on since Moses was quizzed about the commandments dealing with coveting and adultery: "You'll have to talk to my editor."

Eric sauntered down the stairs and the banshee immediately started on him. "How could you print such ugly, horrid pictures? How dare you! They look so ugly. Look at these," she said, poking at the pages again. "These girls look absolutely hideous."

Then Eric cracked his wryest smile and deadpanned, "Those *are* their faces, aren't they?" The angry auntie got this look on her face like she was in a Marx Brothers movie and was supposed to shout, "Well, I never!" Then she stormed out the door. After thanking Eric, I went into the darkroom to see Kate.

Until now, the fact that I had no idea what I was doing with a camera hadn't hurt anyone. But as silly as I thought being a Stampede queen was, the idea that I'd made these girls look so ugly made me feel every bit as terrible as I'm sure the crazed auntie hoped I would. "If my pictures were that awful why didn't Eric send me to take new ones? Why didn't he send you? You're a real photographer," I said to Kate.

"They weren't that bad," she said.

"Didn't you see them?"

Kate didn't bother looking up from her bowl of chemical soup. "Of course I did. You had some really good ones in there."

"But those photos are awful."

Kate grinned. "Yeah, they were. But Eric didn't pick the good ones."

Now *I* looked like the woman in the Marx Brothers movies. Kate laughed. "Eric hates Stampede queens."

# Cowboys Do the Time Warp Again

When Eric handed me my press pass for the Williams Lake Stampede and I read the fine print, I cracked up. A line on the back of a little orange cardboard card read— "Western Dress Only."

It was the first day of the Stampede, one of the biggest rodeos in the world, and I was wearing my everyday outfit—faded Levis, sweatshirt, leather jacket and a pair of camel-brown Wallabees. Not exactly cowboy chic. Not even urban cowboy chic. I had my camera bag slung over my shoulder. I'd finally bought a zoom lens and I was curious to test it out.

Walking across the field to the main ring, I passed a herd of rodeo cowboys in full regalia—jeans, chaps, 10-gallon hats and spangly shirts only a country singer could love.

A burly guard, perfect western material except for the lack of a drawl, stopped me at the gate. "You can't go in there." I flashed my press pass. He pointed at the line on the back. "You wanna go in there, you gotta change."

I tried to convince him that it was a joke. The people who wrote the press pass may have been joking, but he wasn't.

"Them's the rules."

I was already in a bad mood. The day before, Coca-Cola had done the unthinkable and stopped selling Coca-Cola. I'd tried new Coke and it tasted like Pepsi. I panicked. I'd spent almost a hundred dollars buying every bottle and tin of Coke I could find because I was terrified of being unable to write without my daily Coke fix. My closet was full of every container I'd been able to find of "the real thing." This was not the time for a cowboy to be messing with me. But I was officially representing the *Trib*, and the guy was about twice my size. So I wandered off to the fairgrounds to purchase a cowboy hat. It was light brown, made of cheap felt and it set me back eight bucks.

I ditched the jacket in my car, switched into an old denim shirt my mom thought made me look like an escaped convict and tried again. I worked on my posture, slouching so the gatekeeper wouldn't look down at my Wallabees. The cowboy just checked my hat and waved me in. A few minutes later I realized why cowboys don't wear Wallabees. They really don't protect you from the natural hazards of walking in a ring used by healthy horses and monster-sized bulls.

Some people are born cowboys, others have cowboyhood thrust upon them. In Williams Lake, especially at Stampede time, most of the people wearing cowboy hats mean it. Even if they haul logs, file papers or serve burgers for a living, there's something about the Cariboo air that made these folks authentic. It's one thing to play urban cowboy in the city where most folks can't tell a bucking bronc from a donkey with hemorrhoids, but as I moved into the ring to set up my camera, I half-expected someone to dare me to draw.

I realized later that the guard hadn't been joking about the dress code. Kate had a front-page photo of two people in a jail cell. They'd been arrested for the crime of wearing 20th-century clothes and had to stay there until the Stampede Association deemed they'd paid a big enough fine to earn their release.

When I went to the barn dance that night with Liz, Abby, Sarah, Kate and Rick, I wore my cowboy hat—on purpose. And I admit it, I felt kinda cool. When you grow up playing cowboy as a kid, the moment you pop on a stetson, the *William Tell* overture starts playing and you glance down at your pockets for a pair of six-shooters and a pouch of silver bullets. So I suppose the worst part about wearing a cowboy hat was the deep fear that I could get used to it.

Everybody was wearing a cowboy hat that night. And Rick was wearing a beautiful black stetson and the coolest boots I'd ever seen—dark brown leather with an intricate pattern of spurs, six guns and lassos burned in. "Hand-tooled," he told me.

"Do you wear them at your ranch?" I asked.

"Ranch?"

Everyone was staring at me, smiling.

"Aren't you from here?"

Everyone laughed.

"Hell no," Rick drawled. "I'm from Tronna." It took me a second to register he meant Toronto. The most authentic Cariboo cowboy in the office was a city slicker from a slicker city than me.

The barn dance wasn't actually in a barn. It was in the sporting arena, and somehow that fit. There were enough bare-knuckled brawls before midnight to do the O.K. Corral proud. This was the Cariboo equivalent of Mardi Gras, minus the beads and breasts. One big dude in a white Levis shirt with fake mother-of-pearl buttons moved from table to table bumping into people in the hopes of picking a fight. I saw him put down three guys before he finally tagged a bigger dude, who left him on the floor with the remains of his shiny shirt looking like a blood-soaked rag.

The police watched the fights the way they watch players fight at non-Cariboo hockey games. It was a spectator sport, and there was no way they were going to get involved and start a riot.

If you ask any old-timer, they'll tell you the Stampede ain't like it used to be. In the old days, they'll say, the barn dances used to be rough. The dances used to be held in a Native-style longhouse with no roof known as "Squaw Hall." After everyone had downed their first dozen or so beers, the yahoos outside tossed their empties over the wall to land on the yahoos inside. Glass sprayed everywhere, everyone blamed the guy next to him, and mayhem ensued.

The public defender, Lyle Norton, told me about the days

when the jail cells were packed tighter than "hogs in a barrel." (This must have been the official technical term, because Staff Sergeant O'Donnell used it too. So did Eric.)

Everyone knew these things could get out of control and, I suspect, looked forward to the possibility. But flying fists and beer bottles weren't part of a story I felt like I needed to cover. A little before midnight, someone started tossing empty cups at our table. The Toronto Kid, who'd finished several pitchers of beer, shouted the word "asshole." We all waited to see what kind of monster would appear to snap Rick's neck. Nothing did. But the prospect didn't encourage me. So at a little after midnight, this cowboy bid his friends a good night, moseyed on into the parking lot and headed home to the range to catch the end of *Letterman*.

※

The next night there was a party at Eric's, and I arrived just in time to enjoy the black-market barbecued salmon that was caught by a Native for "sustenance" and sold for, well, money for sustenance. Everybody else was already deep into the keg of beer and the locally grown weed. Eric walked up and introduced me to a pretty woman in jeans and a jean jacket who looked a few years older than me. "This is my sister."

Sis took my hand, then leaned close enough to my ear to lick it. "Hi," she slurred. "So you're my brother's new star reporter."

I reminded myself that I was attached. At least I thought I was attached. I hadn't seen Barb since March—and it was now the first weekend in July.

Sis pulled me closer. Her lips were practically inside my ear. I could feel the heat of her breath. What girlfriend? Then she pointed to her brother, my boss, and whispered, "Beat him up. He'll respect you for it."

Not the words I was expecting or hoping for. Kate spotted me and grabbed my free hand. "C'mon."

Eric's sister looked disappointed. "Aren't you gonna beat him up?"

"Maybe we should take off," said Kate.

"Good idea," said I.

And Kate and Abby and I drove downtown to see *The Rocky Horror Picture Show*. We had to know if any of the local dudes would turn up in makeup, corsets and fishnet stockings. We'd all brought cameras just in case. Not a chance. They did take off their cowboy hats though. So much for scoring a cover photo of a cross-dressing cowboy.

As we sat down in the theatre, Kate asked if Eric's sister was trying to pick me up.

"Not quite."

"Good," said Kate. "She's the boss's sister. That's why I thought you could use rescuing. I don't care if you screw around on your girlfriend, but I don't wanna see you get fired."

"Thanks."

"So? What did she say?"

I told her and Kate laughed. "She may not be from the Cariboo," said Kate, "but she's sure got the right attitude."

# No Crime in Crime City

%%

Every year when some bureaucrat sits down to calculate the crime rates across the province, he or she always has a hefty file from Williams Lake. Tina hadn't been lying, the place really did have the highest crime rate in BC.

But there was one brief period in the city's history when crime disappeared. There were no murders, no break-ins, no brawls, no car thefts, not even a traffic accident. And it was just after the Stampede.

As egotistical as this may seem, I was responsible for the disappearance of crime from Williams Lake. But before this sounds like I'm claiming to be a superhero, I should confess that I was responsible for the return of crime too.

Because of all the crimes I stumbled on, the rumour that I owned a police scanner had spread. The police even started coding their transmissions. To be fair, I desperately wanted a scanner, but Eric couldn't convince Stan to buy me one, and I wasn't springing for my own unless I got a raise.

Despite his distaste for me, Staff Sergeant O'Donnell always treated me fairly. Brusquely, but fairly. After the first few months, the police were almost pleasant to me when I popped over to read their press-release book—and they seemed tired enough of answering my questions that they now included one or two answers in their releases. That's why I was so confused the first morning after the Stampede, when I discovered that nothing had happened the night before. Nothing at all.

I asked to speak to Staff Sergeant O'Donnell.

"He's on vacation," the secretary told me. "You can speak to our temporary supervisor, Corporal Swanson."

"That would be great," I said.

And the door opened to reveal my friend Harvey.

"There's nothing in the book today," I said.

"Then I guess nothing happened," he said. And he smiled and shut O'Donnell's door.

The next day the book was empty too. And the day after that. I listened to the radio on the drive back from the police station. Sarah had a story about a robbery at the mall and a suspected arson at the hardware store.

I asked to see Harvey again. "What can I say. It's been a dull week."

"I was listening to the radio this morning. What about the robbery at the mall?" I asked.

"Dunno," said Harvey.

"It was on the radio," I said.

"Guess they got better sources than you."

That night Sarah made spaghetti. She and I knew how to cook three things besides Kraft macaroni and TV dinners. She did spaghetti. I made chili and sloppy joes. As Sarah stirred the pasta, I asked her where she was getting her crime stories.

"Swanson's calling me at the station every morning. It's great. I don't even have to go in and check their stupid book."

Midway through the second crimeless week, I wrote a brief story that Eric ran in a small box on page one beneath the headline "Quiet Lake City."

"According to police press reports, Williams Lake has been exceptionally quiet since the Stampede. The police press-release book reports no crimes of any sort since July 2. 'It's been a dull week,' Corporal Harvey Swanson told the *Tribune*..."

The next morning when I looked through the police press releases, two men had been arrested for a holdup, a car had been stolen and there was a minor fender-bender off Highway 97. No explanations were given, but the great Cariboo crimeless wave had come to an end.

When Staff Sergeant O'Donnell returned to work, he called me into his office to tell me that the police had tallied the statistics and things really were quiet. "It's the only time we've ever handled the Stampede without having to bring in reinforcements from other communities."

So how quiet was it?

"We checked 1,600 vehicles and only 6 people were charged with impaired driving; 112 men and 7 women were arrested for being drunk in a public place; and 3 family members got into a fight with the staff at one of the barn dances."

Staff Sergeant O'Donnell smiled proudly. "It was the best-behaved Stampede ever."

# Cabin of Death

///

"There's been a murder."

Eric looked like someone had just announced he'd scored a raise, won a car and been nominated for a Pulitzer.

I punched the air. I shouted, "Cool!" I was going to cover a murder. Stories don't get any bigger than that.

Eric's grin kept growing. "Three people dead. A shootout." This might be the Cariboo, but this was still Canada. Three people dead. In a shootout. This would be one of the biggest Canadian crime stories of the year.

"Where?"

"The Chilcotin." The Chilcotin was ranch country. One small RCMP detachment covered hundreds of miles. Eric didn't have any specifics. He told me he wasn't supposed to know about this, either. And that was clear when I phoned the staff sergeant at the RCMP's Anahim Lake detachment.

"Who told you that?" he growled, like he'd taken lessons from Staff Sergeant O'Donnell.

"Is it true?"

He grunted.

"Are there really three people dead?"

He grunted again, but this time he muttered too, then swore. I punched the air again, but this time I didn't shout. It was official: I was playing in the big leagues.

"Who-what happened-when-where?"

Maybe I didn't throw the questions all together like that, but I may just as well have, because the answer was the same for all of them: "Can't tell you."

"Why not?"

"Gotta notify the next of kin first. Call me tomorrow."

"I'll call you in half an hour," I said.

"Don't know what I'll be able to tell you then."

"My deadline's 5:30."

"Today?" he asked, sounding genuinely surprised. "Can't you hold this a day or two?"

Now it was my turn to be surprised. "My deadline's 5:30. Sorry."

He swore again and, after I hung up, so did I. Then I turned to Eric. "What do I do?"

"Find a witness," said Eric.

"Can I get out there in time?"

"We don't even know where 'there' is yet," said Eric.

"Shit."

"Just have to find a witness. Somebody's gotta know what happened."

"How?"

"Call everyone in the phone book."

I'd actually done that once before. When I was at the *Province* and war broke out in the Falkland Islands, an editor discovered there were two people from BC on the virtually unpopulated island at the centre of the unexpected and ridiculous war between Britain and Argentina. It was a married couple, and the editor only had a last name—not an uncommon one. He called over Cindy (alias intern number one) and me and said, "Phone everyone in the book with this name. Everyone. And see if we can find a relative who can give us a contact number." It was about eight at night, and there were four or five pages of people to call. Cindy started working backward, I started forward. About two hours later, she scored a family member, a contact number and a conversation with a British Columbian in the Falkland Islands. It was one of the greatest stories of the year and was picked up around the world, because the hubby gave her the type of ironic quote reporters live for. "I moved here because I was convinced

World War Three was going to break out. I figured this would be the safest place on Earth. Nothing here but sheep."

This was going to be a lot easier. There were only two pages of listings for the entire town where Eric thought the murder had taken place. I started dialing.

After half an hour I hadn't found anyone who knew anything—or at least anybody who was willing to admit they knew anything. I called the RCMP again.

"Nothing," he said. "Did you tell the Vancouver papers?"

"No," I said. "Shit," I thought. The story was out.

"Shit," he said.

"I'll call you in half an hour," I said.

He grunted and hung up. "Shit," said I, after I hung up. "The Vancouver papers are on this."

"That's great," said Eric. "If you get it first, you can freelance it."

The only bright side I could think of was there was no way the dailies would take "no comment" for an answer. The RCMP would have to admit something to someone before the end of the day or unplug their phones. We turned on the radio to see if Sarah had anything. I didn't want to call Sarah, just in case she hadn't heard the news yet. It was one thing to share stories, but this was huge.

A half-hour later the RCMP boss still wasn't saying anything, and I was an hour from deadline. But then I scored a rancher who had seen something. "Bodies," he said. "I seen them takin' away the bodies. In an ambulance."

"Do you know who it was?"

"Not sure," he said. "Nobody's sure. Sorry."

He hadn't helped much, but he'd confirmed the name of the ranch. I called the staff sergeant to test my new information.

"Where'd you get that?"

I didn't answer.

"Yeah," he said. And I finally had a "where." But I still needed a "who," a "when," and hopefully a "why" and "how." Three people were dead and I barely had enough information to fill a paragraph.

At 5:30—on my ninth call of the afternoon—the staff sergeant finally gave up the information. He didn't tell me much—just the names and ages of two of the victims—both in their early 20s—and that they'd been shot by an "intruder," who was killed by one of the victims. It really was a shootout.

When I got off the phone I felt so much like Rossi or Kolchak that I actually screamed "Stop the presses!" It would have been more accurate to yell "Stop the typesetters," or "Press the shift key," but this was high drama. Actually, I didn't need to shout anything, because Eric had already announced he wasn't putting the paper to bed until I had the murder. And the next day, Eric was sending me out to get the full story.

After the paper was finally put to bed, Kate pulled me into her darkroom to talk about the murders. I was confused. She'd been in the darkroom all day, but she knew more than I did. She didn't just know the names, she told me what the people did for a living and who they worked for. I wanted to race outside, stop the presses for real this time, and then . . . she was crying.

I asked her why, and she made me promise not to tell. "Swear," she said.

So I did.

Her boyfriend, Jake, had discovered the bodies. Jake owned the ranch the victims worked at. He was their boss. They had been two hours late for work, and since they didn't have a phone, he dropped by to make sure everything was okay.

It was Jake who called the police. The victims were friends of Kate's. She didn't want Eric to know, didn't want Jake to be interviewed, was afraid we'd want to interview her. I was glad she'd trusted me, but wished she hadn't. How could I do the story of a murder at a ranch without interviewing the ranch boss? The more she said, the more I knew; the more I knew, the more I wanted to tell. It's why off-the-record quotes so rarely stay off the record.

That night at the Billy Miner, I ended up in a hot ethics debate with Sarah. She'd heard a rumour about the third name—the one Kate and the police either didn't know or didn't tell me— and even though she couldn't confirm it, she reported it. She'd identified the intruder. Sarah felt we had a duty to tell the story as best we could as quickly as we could, and if the police weren't fast enough with information, it was up to us to find sources who were. I looked at Kate. She looked away.

I said it was too small a community to make mistakes. There was no way I wanted to report rumours about who "may" have been killed. The reporter from the daily paper in Prince George was going with rumours too. So was a Vancouver radio station that had gotten the story from Sarah.

After Sarah left, Kate said she was proud of me. I didn't tell Kate that if the police hadn't told me anything, I would have run with the name of Jake's ranch—even unconfirmed.

I got to work early the next morning, and Eric told me I could relax. It seemed the *Province* had offered Eric big bucks to lead their reporter to the murder site and shoot photos for them. He was taking over the story.

I was furious. And I was relieved. Because I knew that if I went up there, there was no way I could keep my promise to Kate. Of course I would have talked to Jake. And even if he'd said nothing—even if he'd just stood there and cried—I would have reported that.

Eric went to the cabin with the *Province* reporter.

"There was so much blood," he said, when he got back. "So much blood." Then: "It's a great story." Eric had taken as many pictures of the scene as he could, capturing images on colour film for the *Province* and on black and white for the *Trib*. The stories were like the pictures. The big city dailies were full of colour, you could almost see the blood. The *Trib* stories were in black and white. Three people had died. It was a tragedy. I thought Eric's coverage came as close as possible to making a shootout sound boring.

After the big-city dailies left, I regained custody of the murders. The official story was that a trapper had come in, opened fire with his rifle and shot the young couple. The man had a gun of his own and shot back. All three people died. The trapper was crazy. It was probably a robbery gone wrong.

The *Province* reporter found out the trapper was living in Canada under an alias. He was an American fugitive—a killer—and the FBI actually had him on their "wanted" list. His nickname was Crazy Joe. The police found out he'd had a crush on the woman he killed—Kara Bowen. It was the type of story you make movies out of. They headlined it "Cabin of Death."

When it came time for the funeral, Eric wanted Kate to take the pictures. He knew she was going to be there. She refused.

"You have to," he said. "It's news."

Kate walked into her darkroom and shut the door.

Eric wanted to go, but couldn't find out where the service was being held. No one would tell him. It was in a field near the ranch, but Kate never told Eric that. She didn't even tell me until after it was over, after she had helped the families write the obituaries, after they'd scattered the ashes along a path where the lovers used to ride their horses.

"I couldn't do it," said Kate. "Even if it meant losing my job."

Then she told me about going up to see Jake just after the shooting—just after Eric came home from the "Cabin of Death."

While the *Province* was running full-colour photos of the bloodied, bullet-riddled cabin in their weekend edition, Kate and Jake were on their knees, on the cabin's wooden floor, trying to scrub the blood away.

And for the first time since I'd heard the word "murder," I was genuinely shocked. It had never occurred to me before that when a person is killed, someone has to clean up the blood.

# D. B. Cooper Crashes in Cariboo

%%

"He's another D. B. Cooper," said Eric.

"Cool," said I. "Who's D. B. Cooper?"

In case you don't know the answer—because until Eric rolled his eyes and launched into the story, I didn't—D. B. Cooper is the Amelia Earhart of holdup men. And if you don't know who Amelia is, you're on your own.

In 1971 Cooper hijacked a 727, held it for ransom on a Seattle runway and was handed about $200,000 by the airline. Once the plane was back in the air, Cooper bailed out somewhere over southern Washington State or northern Oregon with 21 pounds of $20 bills strapped to his body. Neither his body nor the money were ever recovered. And that's how legends—and folk heroes—are born.

Our would-be D. B., Dale Moodie, was flying a twin-engine Piper Navajo that was chartered by Loomis Courier from Williams Lake to Quesnel—a half-hour trip if the weather was bad, and this was a clear day.

A few miles outside Williams Lake, near McLeese Lake, something went wrong and the plane dove towards the bush.

I heard about this the way I usually heard about such things. Eric had a mysterious tip.

I called the RCMP and asked for Staff Sergeant O'Donnell. O'Donnell wasn't there. It was my pal Swanson who fielded the call.

"I hear there's been an accident out by McLeese Lake."

"Yup."

I waited. He did too. "Can you tell me what happened?"

"Nope." We both waited again.

"Was anybody hurt?"

Another long silence. "You'd have to ask Staff Sergeant O'Donnell about that."

"Do you know what was in the plane?"

"You'd have to ask Staff Sergeant O'Donnell about that."

"Can I talk to Staff Sergeant O'Donnell?"

"Nope."

"How come?"

"He's out at the accident scene."

"Great, so can you tell me how to get there?"

"Can't get there."

"Why not?"

"There's a roadblock."

Uh-huh. "Can I get by the roadblock?"

Yes, you can hear a man smirk: "Only if you get Staff Sergeant O'Donnell's permission."

So when I pulled up to the roadblock, I told the officer that Swanson had sent Kate and me out to talk to Staff Sergeant O'Donnell. Which was sort of true. How else was I supposed to ask him for permission to get past the roadblock?

When O'Donnell spotted me getting out of my Toyota, I was relieved there were witnesses so he couldn't shoot me.

"What the hell are you doing here?"

"Corporal Swanson told me to come out here and talk to you." I really enjoyed saying that. Unfortunately, Kate didn't capture that moment on film because she was too busy snapping shots of what had apparently once been a Piper Navajo.

The wreckage of the plane was still smouldering. I know it's a cliché, but now that I've seen a plane wreck up close, I can tell you that really is what it does. It smoulders, like it's waiting for you to toss more kindling on, so that it can start burning again. Fire crews had spread out to make sure none of the sparks ignited the trees.

Meanwhile, about a dozen volunteers were helping the police search the area, presumably looking for sparks. I wasn't really keen on seeing the burnt body, but I had to ask.

"Where's the pilot?"

"He's gotta be dead," said O'Donnell, his eyes scanning the wreckage.

I did a double take, looking at what was left of the plane, then back at O'Donnell. "You're not sure?" And then it hit me. "He survived? Oh my God, that's incredible!" Now this was a great news story.

O'Donnell looked away from me, scanning the volunteers.

"We haven't found the body yet." Then he barked an order for his people to back away from the remains of the engine in case it blew up. Kate was hovering over the wreck and jumped back with them.

How could they have lost the pilot? The insides of the plane were now the outsides.

Kate snapped more photos—from a distance. I bothered more people for quotes because O'Donnell was too busy to stop me. Then, just as we were about to head back to the office, a pristine city car pulled up and drove a little too close to the remains of the plane. I expected O'Donnell to order it away, but when the doors opened to reveal a well-dressed young couple who looked like tourists in search of a golf course, O'Donnell hustled towards them.

Kate and I assumed they were detectives or official crash investigators—very cool interview subjects—so when O'Donnell was finished with them, I asked him.

"They're from Loomis," he said.

Loomis? That was fast. And weird.

I approached the Loomis man in the city suit, said I was a reporter and asked what the plane was carrying. He barely glanced at me.

"Documents. Nothing particularly valuable." Then he walked away, making it clear he had nothing else to say to me, to O'Donnell, to anyone. Kate snapped a few more shots of the Loomis people in their shiny city shoes, stepping carefully around the melted jigsaw pieces of the Piper Navajo. The couple was looking for something. And it wasn't the pilot's body. I went back to the paper, wrote up the story and told Eric about the strange duo from Loomis. That was when Eric told me who D. B. Cooper was. "Maybe there was something valuable on the plane after all."

"So maybe Moodie bailed out," I said. "Made a run for it."

And even though I pretty much printed the facts as O'Donnell had relayed them, nobody believed what I wrote. Everyone in town had their own theory. "I bet there were gold bars on the plane," said Stan.

"Savings bonds," guessed Lyle Norton.

"Cash," suggested Rick, "at least a million."

It was all anybody wanted to talk about—what happened to Moodie? Why wasn't the body on the plane? What was the real cargo?

The federal ministry of transportation sent an investigator out, and O'Donnell told me about his visit—the day after he left town. I guess it never occurred to O'Donnell that I had a telephone and wasn't afraid to use it—even if there were long-distance charges involved. The investigator, an impossibly officious bureaucrat named Carl, said it would be at least a week before he could comment.

I phoned the Loomis head office and asked again about their claim that there were just "documents" in the plane.

"No money?"

"No money," said their spokeswoman flatly. "Nothing valuable. Just records, papers, things like that."

Kate found out that one of the bags contained photos. Her friend ran a drugstore in Quesnel and was stuck explaining to an irate mom why her party pictures were gone for good. I doubted Moodie had staged the crash to run off with photos of a two-year-old girl covered in birthday cake.

A week later I phoned Carl for his report. He explained in incomprehensible mechanical detail that there was nothing wrong with the plane—at least not before it was spread out all over the forest floor near McLeese Lake.

But what about the pilot?

The pilot was clearly an afterthought. If that. Carl's job was to determine whether something mechanical had caused the crash, and he was certain nothing had. His verdict was "pilot error," and figuring out where the pilot went wasn't his department.

"But you've got to have some sort of theory, right?"

Of course he did. "He wasn't in the plane when it crashed."

I responded like a cartoon character. "What the—"

Carl's theory was that Moodie had fallen out of the plane before it crashed, and that his body must have been swallowed by one of the nearby bogs.

"But how do you just fall out of a plane?"

"Well-l-l-l . . . " he said in a nerdy nasal voice that clearly belonged to someone who never got a date in high school. "Maybe he had to go to the washroom, so he put the plane on autopilot, opened the door to um, pee—and fell out."

If you'd like to pause a moment to reread that, feel free. When I first heard it, it took me a moment to realize I'd actually heard him correctly. I just couldn't believe that the official theory from the government's highly trained crash-site investigator was that the pilot had such a weak bladder that he couldn't hold it in for a 30-minute flight. The gold bars were starting to sound a lot more plausible.

"You think he opened the door to pee?" The physics—and stupidity—of that boggled my mind on so many levels. I remembered the line from the Jim Croce song about not spitting into the wind.

Carl paused, perhaps finally realizing that I was planning to quote him. "Or maybe the door came open, he went back to shut it and he fell out."

And that was that. According to the official investigator from the government of Canada's ministry of transportation, the reason Dale Moodie's body was not found near the plane was that he fell out before it crashed.

The police agreed—although no one else shared the pee theory.

O'Donnell said the body would probably turn up next summer when the marshy areas heated up and hunting season started.

"The body will start to stink pretty bad," said O'Donnell. Yes, rural life certainly does have its charms.

I tracked down a friend of Moodie's, another pilot, who lived in Vancouver. He said it was a tragedy, that Moodie was a good pilot and a good man.

"Do you believe he could have made a mistake and fallen out an open door?" I was not going to ask about his friend's bladder.

"He must have done."

Then, very carefully, in my best Elvis-is-still-among-us-and-playing-in-a-band-with-Jim-Morrison voice: "Do you think there's any chance he's still alive?"

The friend laughed sadly.

"I think he would have called me by now."

The investigation was complete, and the verdict was official: Dale Moodie, 27, of Prince Rupert, BC, was missing and presumed dead. His plane and its cargo, consisting of "assorted documents," had been destroyed.

A week later I got a call from Staff Sergeant O'Donnell. Something was found near the crash site by an old cowboy who'd been hunting in the area: a pocket knife and a belt buckle, which had been identified as belonging to Dale Moodie. Some charred white objects were sent to the RCMP forensic lab in Prince George. It was assumed that the objects were bones. It was news no one wanted to hear.

I recapped all the details, playing up the mystery with the hook that some objects "thought to be Moodie's remains" were sent to a laboratory for analysis. But Eric wasn't feeling mysterious. Maybe he had a bet on when Moodie would be found. My story was vague, but his headline wasn't: "Human Bones Located Near Wreckage Site."

The lab report came back a few days later. The belt buckle may have been Moodie's, but the "bones" turned out to be melted plastic. Eric wouldn't issue a correction, but I had to write a new story that made it look like my original article was wrong.

Nobody phoned to complain though, I think everybody was just as happy as I was that the mystery of the missing Loomis pilot was still unsolved, and that just maybe, Dale Moodie was off in Jamaica buying a round for D. B. Cooper.

# Honorary Woman Appointed

///

I was going home for the Labour Day weekend. My 23rd birthday fell on Labour Day, and I was celebrating by visiting Barb for the first time since I'd left for Ontario.

She'd taken a secretarial job with no weekends off, and to make things more challenging, she was a 6-hour drive to Vancouver that I didn't want to make in the dark . . . or a 10-hour bus trip . . . or a plane ride that someone making $1,150 a month really couldn't afford. But I'd been counting the days until this long weekend since the Stampede. I hadn't even told anyone else in Vancouver that I was coming to town. This wasn't about visiting family or friends. I was on a mission. I'd booked a hotel room, and if all went according to plan, I wouldn't be leaving it until it was time to drive back to the Cariboo.

I was excited, I was horny, I was sneezing and feverish and my mouth was so full of canker sores that it hurt to even think about solid food. I tried to focus on "excited" and "horny."

When Eric told me I looked sick and should go home and get some sleep, I told him I was fine. Actually, I mumbled that I was fine. The cankers blanketed my tongue, so I couldn't really form words.

As soon as I filed my last story, I was going to get in my car and drive straight to Vancouver. I was staring at my computer screen, thinking about the drive and how I was just a few hours away from having sex for the first time in—God, I was too young for it to have been that many months—when I felt a hand on my forehead. My reflexes told me to jump. My body just shuddered.

"JESUS!" It was Kate. "You're on fire."

I turned to deny it and got my hand to my face just in time to avoid coughing on her.

"Go home," she said.

Eric agreed: "Go home."

"Gotta finish this story," I mumbled. And I typed in a few more words about mill closures. Then I took a sip of ice water to numb my mouth long enough to tell Eric, "Better read this carefully. May be a bit . . . Maybe I'm a bit . . ." I couldn't quite pull the thought together.

"Go home," he said.

I drove home, opened the door, Sarah glanced over from the kitchen and reacted like she'd seen a ghost. Apparently, the ghost was me. "You look like death."

"M'fine," I protested through the canker sores. "S'my birday."

"JESUS," she said.

I sniffled, coughed and announced I had to pack. I was driving to Vancouver. I had a hot date. "M'seeing Burb."

"Like hell you are."

I was. I knew I was. And I was about to argue, when my body decided it would be more fun to faint. Sarah grabbed my arm and steered me to my foamie.

"Why don't you just sit for a minute?"

Sitting. Couldn't argue with sitting. I sat. When I woke up, the lights in my room were out. So was the sun. My clock said I'd slept four hours. I knew I had to call Barb. But that required standing. And it took me several tries to pull that off. Fortunately, we'd finally gotten a phone.

"M'sick," I told her.

She swore.

"M'sorry."

She talked, I mumbled.

"Happy birthday," she said. I hung up, stared at the receiver and tried to summon the energy to crawl back to my mattress.

I was starving, but even the idea of eating was painful. Then a car pulled up. Sarah's car. I knew it was her, because I heard her shouting through my door, "You decent?" Before I could mumble my answer, she'd already opened the door.

"Happy birthday," she said. "I thought you could use these."

She was holding a Slurpee—the only thing capable of numbing my cankers so I could eat. I was thrilled. I took a sip of Coke Slurpee. The ice froze my tongue enough so I could manage a "thank you." Then she handed me a bottle of Nyquil. I thanked her again. But she had one more bag in her hand.

"Thought you could use this too. Since your big date's cancelled." She handed me a brown paper bag, grinned. The bag felt heavy. I thought it was food but—

It was that month's *Penthouse*. Madonna was on the cover. I tried to read her face. I was pretty sure it was meant as a gag gift but, considering how I was feeling, it may have been the most thoughtful birthday present I ever received.

It was also the only present I got the day I turned 23, except for a plaque from everyone at the office—a picture of a gorilla with the caption, "You don't have to be crazy to work here, but it helps."

Happy birthday to me.

Naturally, I recovered as soon as it was too late to even think about heading to Vancouver. I drove to town for a Coney burger to celebrate my first day as a 23-year-old, bought a paper at the counter and checked out my story on the mills, the one I'd filed before going home. I just read the front page, not bothering to turn to page six for the end of it. It looked fine. Boring, but fine.

But as soon as I arrived at the office I discovered that as far as Williams Lake was concerned, it was the funniest story ever written. There was one minor typo.

When I was a kid there was a TV show called *Zoom* with a character named "Silent Letter Man" who told you what would happen if you left a single silent letter out of a word. Guess what happens if you leave the letter "f" out of the word "shift?"

The answer is . . . everyone smirks at you for a week and asks you how the mill workers are coping now that management has cancelled their graveyard shits. If not for that typo, I never would have believed people read every word in every article, because it was at the very end of the story—the last paragraph.

※

That night Kate, Abby, Rick and Liz took me to the Billy Miner to celebrate my birthday. They were playing country music—as always—and I found myself singing along to "The Gambler." I now knew all the words. I'd already completely fallen for John Fogerty's *Centerfield* album.

"Sometimes I feel life is just a rodeo" felt like my new motto. I was just thinking I had to get home to the city before I knew the words to every Kenny Rogers song ever written when a word burst out of someone's mouth. It was a word I'd never heard in reference to the *Trib* before—"union."

It dropped onto the table like a, well, like a bomb. And we all sat there silently anticipating the explosion. Finally, someone spoke—hypothetically, of course. "What if we tried to join the Newspaper Guild?" Abby had heard rumours that made everybody but me twitchy. Abby was the highest-paid reporter at the *Trib*. After six years of 60-plus hour weeks, she was making just over $2,000 a month. That might not have been much for a production job, but it was a regal sum for a lowly reporter. The gossip was that the company was going to turf Abby, move me into the "senior" job and hire another ambitious pup to replace me. This, of course, presumed I was planning to stick around for a few years—which I wasn't—but nobody'd bothered to ask me.

Kate was making almost as much as Abby, and she'd been nervous about her job ever since Eric announced he was hiring an "ace photographer." Abby confessed that before I'd arrived, the rumour was they were hiring me to replace Kate. Kate, like

Abby, was one of the hardest workers I'd ever met. She also put in 60-hour weeks and never went anywhere, any time, without her camera.

And now back to those burgers and the word "union" lying there on the table, waiting to detonate. It didn't. It was shoved aside. We started gossiping about other things.

That night I sat by my phone book, contemplating a call to the labour reporter at the *Province*. I knew that if anyone would be able to explain the mechanics and politics of joining the Guild, he would. I knew a union would be good for my friends, but I also knew this wasn't my fight. I thought about how long I wanted to stay at the *Trib* (I'd already put out feelers for theatre jobs back in Vancouver). I thought about how, if I made this call, I'd be branded a "union agitator." And, finally, I decided that while being screwed out of $50 a month might be a good enough reason to skip working weekends, it was not worth risking any future I might want as a reporter. And I put my phone book away.

The next bombshell that dropped was a little smaller. Sarah landed her TV job. It was in Lloydminster—a town that is in both Alberta and Saskatchewan. I'd already started wondering how my little Toyota would like climbing the hill to our place in the snow, so instead of looking for a new roommate, we both gave notice and I started looking for a new place to live.

It was Kate who suggested I should move into the Williams Lake Women's Centre. After all, she'd lived there a few years earlier. The only problem was my gender.

Kate mulled this over a bit, then came up with a solution. She would have the board of directors declare me an honorary woman.

Fortunately, the board of directors consisted of Kate, Liz, Abby and Andrea. They thought it was a great idea. I needed a place to stay, and the Women's Centre could use the extra money. As an added bonus, I'd be sort of like a caretaker or a guard or something, in case anybody was thinking of breaking in and stealing any pamphlets. So the vote was taken, I became an "honorary woman" and moved into the attic of the Williams Lake Women's Centre.

The Centre was a fairly well kept older house, located just off the main drag, only a few blocks from the *Trib* and across from a grocery store where no one thought I'd put their life in danger. The police station, the fire hall and the courthouse were all on the other side of the alley. Not only that, but there was an actual bed in the bedroom. Decadent.

The place had started life as a family home, but was transformed into a halfway house for alcoholics, and then had become the Women's Centre a few years before my arrival. Kate warned me I might get the occasional visit from a Trooper who'd forgotten it was no longer a shelter. It was closed on weekends and it shut on weekdays after five. So I had the run of the place after work as long as there were no late-night meetings. And I was usually warned in advance if anything was scheduled. After all, it would hardly do for a reporter to be in the kitchen heating up frozen pizza while the members of Alcoholics Anonymous 12-stepped through their issues in the next room. But there was nothing to worry about on that count. When the Alcoholics were meeting—Tuesday nights—I made sure I was at the movies. (I called them Chain-smokers Anonymous, because there was always enough smoke during their sessions to set off the alarm and choke me out of my bedroom.)

I also stayed away from the "recovery group for sexual offenders" or, as I lovingly called them, "perverts and scum." For some bizarre reason the Women's Centre had decided to rent their space to a psychiatrist who was treating sexual offenders. There were some objections, since this was the place the women who'd been victims of these men were supposed to go for help. As the reporter who wrote about these creeps I certainly would have objected, since I wasn't keen on having them know where I lived. But the psychiatrist was married to a board member, so I suppose his sessions were at least as legit as my sex change.

※

I met Sarah's replacement while I was covering one of the more interesting non-crimes that had taken place during the great Williams Lake crimeless wave—a typical bar-dance brawl.

When I walked into Judge Turner's court, another guy was already in the press box.

"Steve," he said. "From CKWL."

"Mark from the *Trib*."

"Figured you weren't from *TIME*," he said.

Then Judge Turner entered and it was time to stand.

The case was pretty straightforward. It was the night of the second barn dance, and while Kate, Abby and I were watching Tim Curry do the Time Warp again, a gal named Charlotte was trying to figure out what to do with all her leftover beer tokens. The bar had closed, but she wanted a brew, or at least a refund.

The bartender tried to explain that happy hour was over, but when Charlotte wouldn't quit, he grabbed her arm to lead her away. Bad move. That was when Charlotte's brother, Keith, jumped over the bar rail and landed on the bartender.

In the next few minutes the bartender was bitten, punched and beaten. When a female volunteer moved in to help break up the scrap, Charlotte slapped her. An RCMP auxiliary cop arrived to settle things down and Charlotte kicked him in the crotch.

The trial lasted three days, but there really wasn't much of a defence. At one point, while talking about the volunteer she'd slapped, Charlotte explained to Judge Turner, "The bitch deserved it." And that was pretty much that. It felt less like a criminal trial than an episode of Jerry Springer with Canadian accents. The only argument was over what kind of punishment would constitute justice.

Their lawyer told Judge Turner that poor Charlotte and Keith had suffered enough, and then, with a sense of melodrama straight out of Perry Mason, he announced that having the media in attendance—and he spun to face Steve and I—meant Charlotte and Keith would be publicly humiliated.

"Unless they kill us before we file our stories," whispered Steve.

Keith and Charlotte both glared at us like that was a distinct possibility.

Judge Turner wasn't buying though. They were both convicted of assault, and the judge handed down one of the stiffest sentences imaginable for a Cariboo local. Besides a $300 fine, or 7 days in jail (and 8 months' probation), they were both banned from attending the next year's Stampede.

After the trial was over, Steve and I took off for lunch. It turned out he'd already lived Sarah's dream. He was a TV reporter and now, thanks to budget cuts and some unspecified crime against a network boss, he was in exile in the boonies.

"Is there anything going on in this town?" he asked.

I told him what I'd covered so far. He nodded. "Might be okay, after all."

# *Fear and Loathing in Barkerville*

///

I was certain I remembered having sex with someone prior to arriving in Williams Lake, and since we'd lived together for over a year, I was pretty sure it must have been Barb.

So I was pretty excited when Barb scored two weeks off. She decided to fly to Kamloops—a grown-up logging city about three hours away. Her plane was arriving at eight. I'd pick her up, we'd find the nearest hotel and, um, discuss the complete works of Proust.

She was arriving on a production day, so I knew I'd be busy. On a normal press day, I wrote about a half-dozen stories and a bunch of small filler items like weather updates and regional news briefs. But this wasn't a normal day. Abby called in sick. In the several centuries since she'd been installed at her corner desk—a place I suspected she was actually born—Abby had never called in sick. Eric warned me I'd have to pick up a few extra stories.

I stared at my notes and started turning the latest police brief into something resembling news. I wrote up my forest-fire report. I did a piece on a mysterious restaurant fire. I banged out an interview I'd done with a school trustee on overcrowding. I called Rick Hansen's sister. I could handle a few extra stories. I wasn't worried.

Then the advertising manager came upstairs. The ad manager never came upstairs. He had a nice office that didn't smell of cigarette smoke and ancient coffee grinds. Bald, cheery and much better dressed every day than any of the reporters got when we went out for dinner, Smitty announced he had "great news." Great news? None of us cared what Smitty did. I'd been there three months before I'd seen Smitty in the building. The great news?

"We just had six full-page ads come through, so we're adding another section to the paper today. Isn't that great?"

Today?

Eric started to explain how this wasn't possible. There was no way to fill an extra 12 pages with copy, especially with Abby away sick and . . . Smitty waved a hand like he was wiping all our worries away. "It's okay Eric, I got clearance from Stan for you to put the paper out late tonight. Since it's the long weekend, you can take as long as you need."

And since none of us got overtime pay, "permission" meant Smitty must have gotten Stan to approve overtime for the production crew.

I'm sure Smitty didn't just vanish into thin air, but it seemed like it, because the next thing I remember was Eric growling that I now had six new pages to fill. But where could I find more stories?

"Call city hall," said Eric.

"Abby will kill me." Abby guarded her beats with the type of manic intensity that usually led to fatal crimes of passion in murder mysteries.

"She's too sick to kill you."

I called city hall.

That was the first production day that I didn't go out for lunch. I went across the street, grabbed a taco salad and a two-litre bottle of Coke and ate at my desk.

I phoned city hall and began interviewing people. I didn't even take notes. I typed whatever they said directly into my computer and rearranged their words into inverted-pyramid style. I called for Eric to hand me all the press releases from his inbox. Then I phoned the numbers at the bottom of the pages for fresh quotes, spun those into stories and hit "Send."

I had once thought that writing more than one story in a day was impossible. I'd found out at the *Province* that I was capable of seven. My record at the *Trib* was nine—and several of those were pretty short. That day I wrote stories as fast as Eric could edit them. The final total—when Eric said we had enough to fill the paper— was 23. I clicked "send" at 5:35 and announced I was off for the long weekend. Eric stared at me like he'd just discovered my secret identity. "I knew you were fast but . . . "

I was down the stairs before he could request 24.

The good news was, I was going to make it to Barb's plane in time. The bad news . . . when word spread about how many stories I'd written in one shift, Stan asked Eric again whether he still needed Abby on staff. So the seeds that sparked the union drive may have been planted on the days I took lunch, but they really took root because of the one day I didn't.

After Barb and I discussed a lot of Proust (hey, my Mom's reading this), we decided to visit "historic Barkerville." Barkerville was ground zero in the great Cariboo gold rush (not mile zero—that was Lillooet). Barkerville was the place everybody was rushing to, and thanks to a few government grants to celebrate the province's centennial in 1958, the core of old Barkerville had been reconstructed so tourists could actually enjoy the original Old West experience. You could even pan for gold in an old-time sluice and not find any, sharing the same experience as most of the men who'd travelled hundreds or thousands of miles to find their fortunes and ended up staring at trays full of gravel.

There was a courtroom where an actor, who was likely wondering why he hadn't taken a waiter job instead, performed an extended monologue in the character of Judge Matthew Begbie, the Cariboo's legendary "hanging judge." Apparently Begbie didn't really hang a lot of people. and his rulings seemed vaguely reminiscent of my favourite cowboy-boot-wearing jurist. But Barb wasn't interested in local history, so we left before we found out the verdict in the last case he was recreating.

There was an old-fashioned Barkerville newspaper for sale with actual gold-rush-era headlines. I bought one as a souvenir.

And next to the fake newspaper office there was, appropriately, a "sporting house." When I asked Barb to pose outside the place and she did her flirtiest imitation of a gold-rush madame, vamping in her clingy sweater and clingier jeans, it was time to find a motel and do some sporting of our own.

There are two ghost towns in Barkerville. The reconstructed frontier village is home to the historic cemetery and the genuine frontier ghosts. But that's the quaint tourist ghost town, and even though you know thousands of people died there wondering why they'd ever left their homes in search of gold, it's charming.

The other ghost town is Wells, proudly known as "The Host Town to the Ghost Town." The community held five thousand or so miners in the 1930s, and still had a few thousand people living there until the mine closed in 1967. Now it was home to a few hundred hardy souls, a lot of whom presumably had jobs in Barkerville like pretending to be Judge Begbie. So the town was still there, but all the buildings were empty—except for a handful of stores, a one-room museum and the Jack of Clubs hotel. There was nothing quaint or charming about this ghost town. The broken dreams were too fresh, the paint on people's dream houses just starting to peel. I'd assumed it was a tourist destination. It wasn't. The smart tourists hightailed it back to Quesnel or Williams Lake before dark.

The dozen or so rooms in the Jack were all located over the bar, the only way up was through the bar and you had to check in with the bartender. That would have been fine if I wasn't walking into a bar full of drunk miners alongside a 24-year-old female with long red hair. I'm not sure if these were actually the citizens of Wells, or if the bar was hosting a convention for the type of bruisers who play extras in western-movie bar brawls. I think there were a few women in the bar. I'm sure some of them even had teeth. But all I really remember are the men looking at Barb like they hadn't eaten in weeks, and I kept thinking of the line from "Alice's Restaurant" about "father rapers." During the time it took me to get our room key, Barb turned down a half-dozen invitations for "drinks." As we started up the stairs, she looked at me like she'd seen every ghost in the ghost town.

"Welcome to the Cariboo," I said.

When we got to a room that looked like the place cowboys go to clean up in a small metal tub between gunfights, I knew exactly what was going to happen. I'd seen enough westerns now to realize this was not going to end well. Barb was going to be raped and I was going to be killed—unless this was one of the movies where Clint was a hero and he'd rescue Barb after I was dead and take her for himself. We discussed Proust anyway. Even scary-looking miners can't completely spoil the mood when you're 23. Haven't you ever seen a horror movie set in a small town? But it wasn't the discussing that kept us up all night.

I'd heard stand-ups do shticks about paper-thin walls, but this place had paper-thin floors. We heard everything. The music, the fights, the bottles slamming on the bar. I asked Barb if she wanted dinner. I said I'd go downstairs to get us something. She suggested we buy chips and chocolate bars from the vending machine down the hall. I went to the bar anyway, ordered a couple of burgers and waited—and while I waited, kept my eyes on the stairs back to my room to make sure none of the miners was making their move.

Barb wanted to leave. She was convinced that if we weren't attacked, we were going to burn to death. Everybody downstairs was smoking, the building was made of wood and she was convinced it was a fire trap. I told her she was being paranoid. This hotel had been around forever, it wasn't going to burn down. While we were eating, Barb wanted to know why we weren't just hitting the road. "Where would we go?" We were almost an hour from Quesnel—and that was only if we didn't spend all our time dodging killer Bambis.

"Who cares? Aren't you scared?"

"Sure," I said.

"So why don't we leave?"

"Because then we'd be running away."

"And what's wrong with that?"

I'd seen enough Clint Eastwood videos at Abby's by now to know the answer to that one too, but I hadn't quite figured it out yet.

"This isn't that bad," I said. Then we talked about the police who hated me and the other adventures I hadn't shared during our long-distance calls, and she stared at me like I'd announced I was the official emissary for the Martian Invasion.

"You've changed," she said. It was clear this was not intended as a compliment.

The next morning, The Jack of Clubs was still standing, Barb's honour was still intact, I was still alive and we drove home to Williams Lake.

The next weekend, Kate invited us to Jake's ranch. On the road we spotted wild mountain goats goating their way up a mountain, and Kate showed me how a local passes a bull on a highway. Very slowly.

When Kate took us to the stables, I tried to act like I was a veteran rider. After all, I'd spent almost 10 minutes on a champion roping horse. Barb hadn't been on a horse since she was 10. Kate and Jake taught us to ride. Sort of. "You might be a little sore after," Kate warned us. Gord, a burly 19-year-old ranch hand who looked twice as strong as the horses, set me up on a comatose-looking creature named Buckshot. Buckshot was big, brown and completely innocent-looking—except when he swerved towards low tree branches the same way Jess the trapper had on his tricycle.

Barb landed on a speckled white horse named Sam that didn't try to swat her with any low branches.

Jake gave us a tour of the range—pristine streams, tree-lined paths and endless pasture. Even when Jake and Kate prodded their horses to gallop, they galloped slowly enough that Buckshot could keep up without me flying off the saddle. When I climbed down from Buckshot the ground seemed to be waving, but I felt great. Until I sat.

I thought I'd ached from the hiking trip, but this ride had strained muscles I'm certain just existed for the purpose of being strained. When I managed to stand again, I finally understood why John Wayne walked the way he did. That night Barb and I could both barely move—but we still managed some Proust.

We went out again the next day, and even though everything still ached, I no longer felt like Buckshot was determined to kill me. Barb and I even went for a short gallop on some open pasture. I felt like the Lone Ranger. That night though, I felt more like one of guys in black hats the Lone Ranger takes down with a well-aimed silver bullet.

A couple of guests had shown up for dinner. It took me until we'd finished the soup to realize they were the parents of Kara Bowen, the woman who had been killed in the "Cabin of Death." We talked about the ranch, how much they loved the country, their drive from home, but eventually, inevitably, the conversation turned to the murders.

"I can understand why people were interested," said Mrs. Bowen softly. "I just don't want to talk to them." Mr. Bowen liked the *Sun* coverage. Mrs. Bowen preferred the *Province*. Both were furious at the *Trib*. Eric's stories were mild compared to the two dailies, as bland as one could possibly make a triple killing with a fugitive from the FBI involved. It was all just-the-facts-ma'am, straight-ahead reporting. But it was local. All their friends read it. And that made it real.

Gord wanted to kill Eric for taking the pictures. "He had no right. If I'd have seen him I would've knocked his head clear off right then."

And as he said that, Kate and I both knew that it could have been her taking those pictures, that if it wasn't Jake's ranch, it would have been. And that if Eric hadn't wanted the extra money, it would have been me staking out the cabin, snapping photos, trolling for much more graphic quotes and images than Eric had settled for. But it was Eric, and that made Eric evil.

Everyone else felt pretty much the same as Gord. They appreciated the coverage of the "mad trapper." They were impressed at how the *Province* dug up his criminal history. But they didn't understand why their daughter's death couldn't have been left alone. I wanted to defend Eric, defend my job, but this wasn't the time for a journalism-school ethics debate on the "public's right to know."

How do you explain the concept of "newsworthy" when you know in your heart the honest translation is really just "a good read"? And how did writing about a triple murder where everyone ended up dead serve the public good? So as they argued about the coverage, I stared at the steak on my plate and imagined how I would have written the story. And I knew that if they wanted to hurt Eric, they would have wanted to kill me.

That night I didn't feel like discussing Proust.

# Cold Snap
# Freezes Lake City

///

When I first started at UBC, my friend Tom and I went to take a ride off campus. I can't remember where we were going, but I do remember that we stopped in front of his car, because I noticed something wrong with it. It was a turquoise 1970 Volkswagen station wagon that still had its Alberta plates, and something that looked like an electrical plug sticking out of its front end.

"What's that?"

"A plug," he said, as if it was a stupid question.

"I know that. But what's it for?"

"For the block heater, for the winter," he replied, like I was a moron. And I felt like a moron, because I'd never heard of a "block heater."

Tom explained.

"You mean you have to plug in your car in the winter?"

"Yeah," he said, sounding a little defensive.

Then a question that no Canadian except a born Vancouverite could ask with impunity: "Why?"

"Because it's so cold that otherwise the engine could freeze." I was sure this was some kind of strange Albertan humour, but when it became apparent from Tom's face that he really did plug in his car in the winter to keep his engine from freezing and shattering, I burst out laughing. "Why would anyone live somewhere you have to plug in your car?" Like I was saying, I don't remember where we went, but I do remember that it was an awfully quiet drive.

For those of you who have never lived in Vancouver, we have a delightful system for handling winter. With rare exceptions, we keep all our snow up on the nearby mountains where it belongs, and when we feel like skiing or snowboarding or hiking, we drive up to the mountains to visit it. Yes, we do get too much cold winter rain and sometimes we get a few inches of snow that cripples traffic for days but, for the most part, our snow knows its place. Most Vancouverites watch winter-weather stories on TV about blizzards in Ontario or frozen pipes bursting in Saskatchewan like they're science fiction—or comedy—and then we head outside to play tennis.

When I saw Thomas's car plug I knew at last that I was not from the Real Canada. Real Canada is where people wear sweaters for survival, not style.

I know Williams Lake was Real Canada because, despite a lack of snow, it hit -42°C in November. It was the coldest November day on record, beating the 1970 and 1978 records of -28 and—lucky me—I was there for it. And it didn't feel much warmer inside the Women's Centre than it did out. Before the brutal attack of my first Real Canadian winter, if someone had asked me what a person does when it hits -42, I would have responded, "Turns blue and quickly dies." I was only half wrong.

The day winter hit like a ton of ice, I walked the 10 blocks to work. By the time I arrived, the only way I knew the number of fingers and toes I possessed was from memory. My beard was covered with icicles, and I felt like the poster boy for an anti-freeze campaign.

In case you're wondering why someone would be crazy enough to walk 10 blocks to work in the kind of weather that freezes the moisture on your eyeballs, it's because that morning, when I went outside to start my car it just made this sickly little choking noise. Actually, it sounded more like chuckling.

At noon I called the repair shop, asked them to tow in my sick little Toyota and do whatever was necessary to revive it. I also walked to the nearest clothing store and invested in some thick woollen long johns. Up until then, the only kinds of long johns I'd ever bought were topped with chocolate frosting. I felt silly as I went into the changing room and shimmied into my new wool undies, but as I walked outside and my legs remained approximately body temperature, my embarrassment vanished as fast as a snowman in a Chinook.

Back at work, everyone was talking about the weather. "Yup, it's pretty bad for November," said Gus, one of the *Trib's* ancient pressmen. "But this ain't nothing. I remember one winter when it went down to -60." In spite of my woolly underwear, flannel shirt and bulky Cowichan sweater, the concept of -60 sent a shiver down my spine. "Of course," Gus continued, "that's not counting the wind-chill factor."

It was a good thing I hadn't had lunch yet.

That afternoon I did a story on the effects of the weather. Pipes were freezing, cars (other than mine) were refusing to budge, the mills were cancelling shifts.

At about 4:30, I talked Kate into giving me a ride to the repair shop. They said my car was fine and handed me the bill. When I saw my faithful little Toyota I almost wept. There, poking out of the front grille, was a little rubber cord with a plug at the end. I think it was laughing at me.

A few days after my car was first plugged in, I walked across the street to the corner store to buy my minimum daily cola requirements. I was amazed at how warm it was—I even took off my toque and scarf, and unzipped my coat so I could enjoy the breeze.

When I returned home I clicked on the radio and a few minutes later heard " . . . and it's -16 in downtown Williams Lake."

And I thought it was warm. I was officially a Canadian.

# Death of a Trooper

///

Alice Willow was worried about the weather too, and I suspect her car already had a block heater. Alice was a Native woman who radiated motherly concern and had enough lines on her face that it was obvious she didn't find out how tough life was by reading about it in a textbook. A street worker based out of the Friendship Centre, Alice was worried the cold snap was going to kill one of the Troopers. Being new to Williams Lake, I asked what happened most winters.

"Most winters," said Alice, "somebody freezes to death." That's when I discovered that in Williams Lake, "the other side of the tracks" wasn't just a quaint expression—it's where most of the Troopers lived. In cardboard lean-tos.

Alice thought a story might prompt a solution. Or at least a discussion. She knew there wasn't enough room in the jails for them, and the Friendship Centre wouldn't admit anyone who'd been drinking, because they didn't have the staff to handle drunks.

But something had to be done. With temperatures averaging -30, it was too cold for anyone to survive out there.

"What if someone gets drunk and stumbles and doesn't make it back to their place?" she asked.

"Could that really happen?"

"Almost every year," she said. "Almost every year."

I wrote and filed a story about Alice's concerns. When I opened the paper the next day, it wasn't there. It had been bumped. It was bumped again the next week. There were city hall budgets and school board speeches. It's not like Troopers were news. I'm not sure the story ever would have made it into the paper if one of them hadn't frozen to death.

Tommy Dawson wasn't considered a full-fledged Trooper. He still had a home that he went to sometimes, a family that let him stay in the basement when he was sober enough. But most nights he slept on the streets or in the lean-tos. One Monday night Dawson left the bar and was walking to the other side of the tracks when he slipped down the hill.

He was found by a railway employee early the next morning. He was still alive when he got to the hospital, but he'd been out in the cold too long to be saved.

I phoned Alice for her reaction.

Her reaction was to ask why my story hadn't run yet.

I rewrote my original article, changing all her concerns from our earlier interview to past tense. Then I told the story of Tommy Dawson.

I asked Eric for permission to go to the funeral, talk to Tommy's family and friends and write about the death of a Trooper. I told Eric I wanted to do something significant, a long feature that might alert people to the need for a shelter so no more Tommy Dawsons would freeze by the railway tracks. Eric thought it was a great idea. "It's the kind of story that wins awards," he said.

I remembered a conversation I'd had with Staff Sergeant O'Donnell. We were talking about an elderly Native who'd been reported missing. O'Donnell told me he'd learned to accept that many missing people, especially older Natives, would never be found. Sometimes, he said, people wander off because they know their time has come "so they just go someplace to disappear."

I'd like to think Tommy Dawson was wandering like that when he stumbled by the railway tracks. I'd like to think there was some poetry in his death, some meaning, but I never found it.

The day of the funeral, the fire chief decided to hold a press conference to show off a new hook ladder. I wanted to go to the funeral, but everyone else was busy. Eric said someone had to cover the press conference because the firemen were going to be wearing their dress uniforms.

"People love firemen," he said. "Just make sure you get lots of great pictures."

I got pictures of the firemen, but there would be no great pictures of Tommy Dawson's funeral. No pictures at all.

So I never did write about the death of a Trooper. Until now. All we had was a simple little obituary on the back pages where deaths like that usually go—if they're acknowledged at all.

# Cowboy Theatre

*%*

PLEASE CHECK YOUR GUNS AND KNIVES AT
THE DOOR.

That's the first sign you see when you walk into the bar in
Alexis Creek. The words were written with black felt marker on
white cardboard. Some city bars might have signs like that for
ambience, but this was cowboy country.

Next to the mounted trophy head of one very large ex-moose
was another sign: IF YOU VALUE YOUR LIFE AS MUCH AS WE
VALUE OUR TROPHIES—LOOK DON'T TOUCH. I think the high-
calibre insurance policy was a joke, but I still wouldn't try to
touch their moose.

A steer skull was mounted beside it, and someone had put red
light bulbs in the eye sockets.

In the bar, the Natives sat in the bottom section. The White
folks sat at the top. It was so clearly segregated that I asked one
of the cowboys if there was a rule about it.

"There's no rule," he said. "That's just the way it is."

A two-hour drive from Williams Lake, Alexis Creek wasn't
exactly John Wayne's Old West. There were no shootouts on the
dusty streets. The locals had satellite dishes and glossy magazines.
And if they waited a day or so, they could snag the national edition of the *Globe and Mail* at Pigeon's General Store.

But one thing they didn't get in Alexis Creek was live theatre.
Outside of elementary school Christmas pageants, live theatre
didn't exist. That's what Anton told us one night after we'd finished
our rehearsal. Anton was the owner of the store in Alexis Creek.

Anton was also a schoolteacher, a pilot and the director of the Williams Lake Players' Club production of *The Apollo of Bellac*.

"Most of them don't know anything about theatre," he warned us. "They won't have any idea how to behave or what to do."

As small towns go, Williams Lake had a fairly grand theatrical tradition. Gwen Pharis Ringwood, one of Canada's first internationally acclaimed playwrights, was a Williams Lake local, and she had died just two years before I arrived. Everyone in the Players' Club had worked with her, and she'd inspired them to take their theatre seriously. How many community theatres have a Broadway playwright on their board? But when Abby suggested I audition for a show with the Players' Club, I was still expecting Neil Simon or Agatha Christie, not Jean Giradoux.

But Giradoux it was, and I was cast as "the Apollo" in *The Apollo of Bellac*. In the play, a mousy young woman (played by a young gift-store clerk named Tracy) is applying for a job with a mysterious corporation. All the men ignore her and she has no idea how to get their attention until a strange inventor, the Apollo, reveals the secret of success: pandering to male vanity. All she has to do is tell men how handsome they are, and they'll fall over themselves attempting to do her bidding.

The cast was made up of teachers, a few civil servants and me. Our show played alongside two equally obscure comedies in the Overlander ballroom, and all were served alongside a roast-beef buffet. Our crowds were always enthusiastic—and flattering. So when Anton suggested we "tour," the show to Alexis Creek the verdict was unanimous. The only problem was that there were a half-dozen walk-on parts for "handsome men," and some of our handsome guys couldn't or wouldn't make the trip just to walk across the stage. But Anton had a solution. He'd draft some extras from Alexis Creek.

A stage was set up in the town hall. The space also served as the court when Judge Turner made the rounds, so it wasn't entirely new to theatre. Again, the performances were scheduled as dinner theatre. Since we were special guests and there was nowhere else to eat in town that night, because everyone was coming to the show, we actually got to eat with the audience and share the main course before going on stage for dessert.

Everyone was dressed in their Sunday best, and, unlike the bar, White folks and Natives sat side by side. While the audience was served fresh pie, the cast was smeared with fresh makeup.

During a run-through that afternoon we met our walk-on co-stars. Killer cowboys who I am certain were steely-eyed when faced by charging bulls were clearly terrified by the prospect of walking across a 16-foot stage. Makeup wasn't an option with these swaggering dudes.

The shyest by far was a huge guy, maybe six foot six. He had a proper cowboy name like Tex. And he looked like he could take Clint Eastwood squint for squint. But when it came time for the show, Tex was struck with a fear so primal that only his cave-dwelling ancestors could have fully understood it. He didn't just freeze, I think he died and went directly to rigor mortis.

I was on stage hiding behind a prop pillar, but I heard Anton's increasingly panicked whispers as he tried to prod Tex on—and considering where we were, maybe they used an actual prod—because there he was. Somehow, through some supreme triumph of will, Tex kept his legs moving long enough to make it all the way across the stage. Tracy didn't even have a chance to say how handsome he was before the audience burst out cheering for good ol' Tex.

When our other walk-ons came out to do their thing, the audience shrieked their approval. Each of the extras received an ovation that would have made Pavarotti blush.

As I launched into my speech about how every man, no matter how unattractive, is actually handsome, one old rancher hollered, "Are all you ladies listening to this?" Then, pointing towards me, he said, "This guy's right, you know. Shore is."

By the end of the play, everyone in the cast was grinning no matter what our roles called for. The audience didn't know that in theatres, you're supposed to sit still and shut up. That's what made their applause so special. It wasn't something they knew they were supposed to do. They meant it.

After the show we all retired back to the bar, the town's real cultural centre. It was early Sunday morning before any of us drifted upstairs to our rooms. I was one of the stragglers, and when I finally got up to leave, Tex was still at the table, nursing a hefty beer and smiling as proudly as if he'd just won an Academy Award. I'd betcha anything that one day Tex will be sitting around a table just like that when he tells his grandchildren about the good ol' days, when he used to be an actor.

# Politician Caught
# in Videogate

The police thought I had a scanner. Eric's theory was that news followed me around. He came up with that theory when Kate took her vacation, Abby moved into the darkroom and I took over her coveted city hall beat—and all the rest of the reporting.

I had three weeks to cover city hall. So, naturally, that was when we broke the biggest political scandal in years. It began with Eric getting one of his tips. According to Eric's source, Alderman Jeremy Kane had spent the night in jail in Vancouver. I never found out where the tip came from. I'm not sure I wanted to know—it would have destroyed Eric's mystique. Although if I had to guess, I'd say there was a reason everybody but me called Staff Sergeant O'Donnell "Glenn."

Three phone calls later we had our story, or the start of one. Alderman Kane had been convicted of making a false declaration. When he wasn't aldermanning, he ran a video store, and he'd undervalued some tapes he'd brought across the border from Seattle. The sentence was a day in jail and a $6,000 fine. The tapes were confiscated. It was all pretty straightforward. If he wasn't an alderman, we wouldn't have cared. They weren't even dirty movies.

Kane was out of town, so we couldn't get a response from him. Maybe if we'd been able to reach him and get a quote, I would have stopped there. But he wasn't returning our calls and that meant we had to figure out another way to fill several inches on page one without rehashing his political history, a history I didn't happen to know. When I was working at the *Ubyssey*, Nancy said I was like a pit bull puppy. "I know you're just being playful, but once you get your teeth into a story you don't let go. You don't need editing," she said, "you just need a leash." So when Nancy had a story, she'd point me in the right direction and say "sic 'em." That's how she set me loose on the student council president about the SUB building fees. And that's pretty much what Eric did with me and the Kane story.

I can't remember who asked it first, Eric or me, but we wondered whether someone could still serve in public office if they'd done jail time. A call to the city clerk's office elicited what I considered an evasive answer. It could have been sincere confusion, but it's hard not to be suspicious when there's a local politico's head on the block. So Eric and I started playing telephone tag with various provincial officials until Eric hit the jackpot when he discovered that "if it was an indictable offense, he has to resign."

I called Kevin Holland at the Crown counsel's office for definitions and confirmed that this was, indeed, an indictable offence. And Kane had been indicted. He'd gone to jail. Then it was back on the phone to the Attorney General's office to confirm this. The legal advice we got from the bureaucrat on hand was that Kane could no longer remain an alderman.

Eric and I jammed together the story. Page one. Alderman Jeremy Kane had been convicted of customs fraud and, according to the law of the land, had to resign.

The next morning when I stopped by the convenience store across from the Women's Centre there wasn't a *Trib* to be found. I thought maybe the delivery van was late. "Sold out. It's the Kane story," the clerk explained. "Everyone wants to read it."

When I got into the office, I had several messages from Kane. Now he wanted to talk. "I have no intention of resigning," he told me. He offered his version of what had happened and explained that it was all a misunderstanding.

But he was a politician and I was a reporter, and that meant it was my job to assume he was lying. I was determined to keep at him, and Eric was determined to keep the story on page one until we got a resignation letter. Eric explained that Kane was the mayor's right-hand man, so this would seriously shake up the balance of power on city council. I didn't know anything about Kane or the mayor or what power was balancing where. I'd paid no attention to municipal politics since I'd arrived. That was Abby's beat.

I'm sure Kane assumed the paper and the public would get bored of the story—but I didn't. Covering a scandal was a lot more fun than covering pronouncements on water-main repairs and tax levies. And the longer the mayor ducked my calls, the longer the story was going to stay alive. Then, right at the end of my three-week tenure as city hall reporter, the mayor finally agreed to talk about Kane. She kept circling away from the issue, but I kept repeating what I'd heard from the Attorney General's office. Then I asked what she planned to do at the next council meeting if he failed to resign.

"I guess I'll have to call for him to be dismissed," she said.

Then it was my turn to circle away from the topic and get her off the phone before she started hedging and clarifying. By the time I hung up, I'd written my lead. Stan was upstairs visiting Eric, so I called through the hole in our wall and announced Thursday's top story: "Mayor Lawrence says if Kane doesn't resign, she'll oust him herself."

The next week, Kane announced his resignation—right after the paper had gone to bed. He told Steve he wanted to give the radio an exclusive, and that he wouldn't grant the *Trib* any interviews because he blamed "the media" for hounding him from office. Kane blamed me.

After it was all over, I finally apologized. To Abby.

I felt like I'd stolen her story. This was her beat and I'd not only covered the big scandal, I'd scored what every journalist has dreamed of since Watergate—I'd forced a politician to resign.

I thought Abby would hate me—but she didn't. "I'm happy it was your story," she said. "I always thought Kane was one of the good guys."

# "No Indians Allowed"

%%

I'd heard people talk about "land claims" before. It was the type of thing you talked about in the campus pub when you worked for a university paper—land claims, the US in El Salvador, apartheid in South Africa and whether it was right for pop companies to sponsor rock concerts. We took these things seriously. We were university students who worked for the student paper; we took everything seriously. But "land claims" in Canada didn't seem any more real or relevant in Vancouver than the US in El Salvador.

In the Cariboo, the issue of land claims wasn't an abstract concept. Just about everybody would be affected by any settlement. Non-Natives would lose their homes, their jobs, their lives. The Natives could reinvent their lives. When Eric sent me to cover a forum at city hall, I assumed it was going to be a dull debate with a half-dozen people watching. But the place was packed, tempers were flaring and I realized Eric might have sent me there in case a fight broke out. Tempers really lit up when one chief launched into a passionate speech explaining that these were not "land claims" because the land had never belonged to the White man. I thought he was articulate, brilliant and, finally, a paranoid freak, because he went off on some bizarre tangent about how the White man had waged "germ warfare" against his ancestors. I told Eric about this the next day and how I wasn't sure how to write this up, since the chief was clearly unbalanced.

"He was probably talking about the epidemics—smallpox, flu . . . " he said.

"Epidemics aren't germ warfare," I said.

"They can be," said Eric. I looked at Eric like he'd lost his mind, and Eric looked at me like I didn't have one. "Natives didn't have any resistance to European diseases."

"Yeah," I said, "everybody knows that."

"So when people died of smallpox or influenza, the White settlers bundled up the victims' blankets and clothing and instead of burning them like they normally would, they traded them or gave them to the Indians."

"They knew they were infected and they—"

Eric nodded. "Germ warfare."

I couldn't believe it, so I looked it up at the library. I don't know if free blankets were the factor in the Cariboo, but the Native population in Williams Lake dropped from 3,000 in 1862 to just 500 a few years later. My high-school teacher had definitely missed that detail when I studied Canadian history.

In 1985, things were a bit more subtle.

The biggest story I wrote for the *Trib* was sparked by an impassioned letter to the editor. Julie Jacobs wrote to tell us that her boyfriend, Russell, had seen a vacancy sign in front of an apartment building, so he dropped in to speak to the landlord. Russell told Julie she should visit the place and take a look. The vacancy sign was still posted, but when the landlord opened the door this time, he informed Julie that the apartment had just been rented. A week later the sign was still up. There was an apartment for rent to a White man like Russell, but not to Julie, not to a Native.

So that was the story. It was a straightforward investigation of a bigoted landlord. I called Julie, spoke to Russell, and then visited the landlord, who claimed it was a misunderstanding. Julie, who still had to find an apartment after months of searching, was close to tears as she told me, "Things like this shouldn't be allowed to go on." It was sad, but Eric didn't think it was news—especially since we couldn't prove anything.

It was a trip to the Friendship Centre that complicated things.

I told Alice Willow about Julie, and she let loose a hefty sigh. "That sort of thing goes on all the time."

I know it was naive of me to be surprised.

"Most landlords consider Indians bad tenants so they won't rent to us. They see an Indian coming and the 'No Vacancy' sign goes right up."

"So where do Indians live?"

"Let me take you to the palaces." And the way she said "palaces" I knew they weren't going to be fit for royalty.

We got in my car, drove to the railway tracks and followed them to the edge of town. She pointed at something that looked like an abandoned barn and something else that looked like a storage shed: "The palaces."

"Guess what the rent is for that one? It's got no electricity and no running water."

It hadn't occurred to me there would be rent for something that looked like that. I assumed it was abandoned. The total rent for the house with Sarah had been $425, and I was paying $250 for my room at the Centre. This couldn't be that much, but it had to be something outrageous for Alice to be so upset. "Two hundred?"

"Six hundred and fifty."

That's when Alice told me about the Bajardi family. The Bajardis made a living renting slum housing at penthouse prices. "Sometimes the tenants are drunks," said Alice. "Sometimes they are 'bad risks.' But mostly they're just people who can't find anywhere else that'll take them.

"There are babies being raised in these places," she said. "There are people who moved here from the reserves looking for a better life."

A better life? The firemen were burning nicer buildings to test their hoses.

"Some people like it here," Alice said. "It's like the reserve. If you don't want to keep things clean, it's okay. If you want to get drunk and tear the place up, it's okay. But other people, well, they just have no place else to live." So I kept driving and Alice kept listing the rental rates. Five hundred for a shack. Eight hundred for a sprawling barn that looked ready to collapse.

She offered to take me visiting. I met a single mother with her infant son and a teenaged boy who was caring for his bedridden, dying grandfather. I felt like I'd stepped through a mystic portal into a third-world village.

The locks on some doors were padlocks, like woodsheds. And they only locked on the outside, so people could lock them when they were leaving but not when they were at home. There was no heat and no insulation in a town where the temperature could drop to -42. Some palaces had electricity, some had plumbing, but the only thing they had in common was they were all hell-holes and they all cost more to rent than a nice apartment in downtown Williams Lake.

I wanted to get the Bajardis.

I went to the police.

It turned out the Bajardis had been in trouble with the law before, but nothing ever stuck. Assorted charges had been laid, but usually the complainants or witnesses were "less than reputable."

Alice's co-worker, Phil Lacroix, the Native court liaison, explained that Natives weren't generally great witnesses. "Most of us don't trust the legal process," explained Phil. "So if these people have a problem, they don't like to call the police."

I asked Phil if he'd ever had trouble finding a place.

"Yeah, but listen to me. I don't sound Indian, do I? So I can call up first, see if the place is still for rent."

"And if they don't rent to you, then you can sue them?"

"Yeah," he said. "As long as I don't mind renting from an asshole."

A few weeks after our grand tour, Alice took me to visit some people who used to live in the palaces. They'd found places in the city, but none of them wanted to make waves. They were too afraid that if they upset anyone, if they drew attention to themselves, they might lose their new homes. They'd only allow me to interview them if they could use pseudonyms. No photos. "Charlie," a 35-year-old father of three, had entirely surrendered on the concept of justice; he just wished there was some honesty. "If those apartment people don't like Indians, they should just say, "No Indians allowed" in the paper and they wouldn't hurt us. We wouldn't even bother them. Some of these places, they say "no kids" and you wonder if they really mean "no Indian kids." These landlords, they don't know I don't drink. They just look at my colour."

Alice said she'd spoken to two aldermen about the Bajardis but, as far as she knew, the issue of slum housing had never been officially raised by city council.

I asked Abby about it.

"No one wants to talk about that stuff," she said. "City council won't go near it."

"Have you ever written about the Bajardis?"

"I tried to. Years ago."

"What happened?"

"I got a warning. If I wrote anything about the Bajardis I'd get hurt."

"From who?"

"Never found out exactly."

"Is that why you let it go?"

"No one wanted to talk. No one would complain. No one. How can you help people who don't want to be helped?"

Then Abby told me who handled zoning bylaws and wished me luck. The zone drone acknowledged the "houses" were substandard, but claimed that if no one forced the issue there was nothing he could do.

No one at the fire department would acknowledge these people were living in fire traps. At least not on the record.

Off the record, I had all sorts of officials tell me that although what the Bajardis did was technically against the law, they couldn't build a case if none of the tenants were prepared to press charges.

I finally wrote a two-part feature about the slum landlords and the legitimate landlords who allowed them to exist. There was no way to point a finger at the Bajardis without risking a libel suit.

At least I had photos—people would see . . .

"Can't use 'em," said Eric.

"You mean Stan won't let us. Don't tell me the Bajardis advertise with us."

"You can't call a place 'a slum'—you need someone else to say it. Someone official to take the heat. Or the Bajardis can sue us."

Eric agreed to let me write a column about the palaces—as long as I didn't identify the locations or the owners. He let me write the editorial too. I compared the situation to apartheid, said that if racial segregation was wrong in South Africa, it was wrong in Williams Lake. I laid the blame on the legitimate landlords, the ones who slammed their doors on all the non-White faces. Our advertisers. Our readers.

This was a little different from our typical right-wing editorials—like the one demanding an end to universal health care.

I braced for calls, letters, screaming banshees.

Eric smiled when I told him what I was hoping for. It was a sad smile. "Nobody's going to want to talk about this," he said. "That would mean they might have to do something. Bet you win an award for these, though. It's good work."

In the week after the stories were published, the *Trib* received a grand total of one letter to the editor about the series—a short note from a woman who wrote, "It's hard to believe that stuff like this happens."

Alice called to say her co-workers at the Friendship Centre were pleased. "Never thought they'd let you write it," she said. "Never thought the *Trib* would print it."

"It didn't do anything," I said.

"The *Trib's* never written about us like that before," she said. "That's something."

Lyle Norton, the public defender, called me into his office to talk about my articles. He liked them, but said it was a good thing I hadn't mentioned the Bajardis by name. "That was smart of you."

"I wasn't trying to be smart, I just couldn't find anyone who would name them."

"Not surprising," said Lyle.

"Do you know anyone who would talk?" I asked.

"You sure you want to find someone?"

"Of course I do."

"Be careful with this. These people don't hire lawyers. They don't write letters to the editor. If they don't like your story, you'll find out when they sneak up behind you with a steel pipe."

I still can't believe I said what I said next, but I couldn't shake the image of that boy with the dying grandfather. "Maybe if I actually get hit, at least there'd finally be someone willing to press charges."

Lyle didn't laugh, didn't even smile. "You ever thought of buying a gun?"

A few weeks later, Alice called. She had a live one—a young, single mother who was stuck in one of the palaces. Alice and I drove to meet her. Delia was waiting outside something that looked like an outhouse—and not a nice one. Her 10-year-old son, Danny, was standing beside her, bouncing a soccer ball on the dirt. Delia was paying $450 a month, because no one else would take her. But now that she'd spent a few nights in the place, she was afraid to stay.

It was a three-room shack. The bedrooms were hardly the size of closets. The walls weren't much thicker than a typical issue of the *Trib*. I wanted a picture, something that would get across how small this place really was. I asked Danny to lie on the floor of his bedroom. He wasn't a tall kid, but when he stretched out his body covered the entire length of the room. He couldn't spread his arms without hitting both walls. The fake-wood panelling had warped so badly that there was a gap Danny could crawl through between the kitchen and the bathroom. The gas stove looked leaky, the fridge probably couldn't keep anything cold without ice packs. There was electricity, but loose wires criss-crossed the ceiling like cobwebs, and I had to duck to avoid them.

Delia was scared that if her social worker came to visit, he might take one look around and declare her an unfit mother.

I told Eric the story and he was ready to go with it. If Delia would sign a deposition, he was prepared to let me cut loose with a front-page attack that named the Bajardis. He'd even run the photos. "They're great," he said. "Really disturbing. Hard to look at these and believe this is Canada."

I didn't like the idea of being attacked. I was scared. But I had to tell this story. If I couldn't write a story about slum landlords endangering people's lives, then I wasn't really a journalist, was I?

I called Alice with the good news.

Silence. A long silence. Then . . .

"We're gonna have to find another one." Delia had called Alice a few days after our interview. It turned out she'd been evicted from her last apartment because of a bounced cheque. Delia was a "bad risk," and she was afraid that if this story was published and mentioned her name that would come out and she'd be homeless again. And this time no one would rent to her. "She's a good mother," said Alice. "She's straightened herself out. And your story will probably bring in someone from the Ministry with a court order to take away her son."

I wouldn't have blamed the social worker if they took Danny away now. How could a kid live in a place like that? How could anyone?

"We'll have to wait," said Alice.

"Yeah."

"Someday somebody will turn up."

"Yeah."

I always figured the reason my story faded away as quietly as it did is that while the good citizens may very well have agreed that the palaces were terrible, most of them were still relieved that there weren't going to be Natives moving in next door.

At least they weren't handing out smallpox blankets.

# "Human Pâté"

%%

There's something about being a reporter that makes a person just a little bit stupid. That's my excuse anyway. But if one reporter is stupid, add another and their combined IQs drop by half. At least that's what happened whenever I got together with Steve. The first time I visited the Press Club in Vancouver, it was clear to me what it was really designed for—so that no one else would ever have to drink with journalists. But Steve would have been fun to hang out with even if he wasn't my official competition. The proper response to one of Steve's jokes was a shocked laugh followed by a feeling of deep shame and a disgusted cry of "That's sick!"

Steve was the one who told me about "Cariboo public transit": "Head over to the Lakeview"—which was, naturally, the only hotel in town without a view of the lake—"check out the parking lot, hot-wire a car, pick up all your friends, drive it out to the ranch, farm or reserve and torch it."

The first time we covered an abuse case together, Steve dubbed the Cariboo "Canada's Ozarks."

So when Eric told me I had to check out a major accident on Horsefly Road—"A pickup and a logging truck. Two people dead. I want you to go out there and get pictures"—I thought "if I really have to do this, I'm going with Steve."

I didn't get it, though. We never ran accident photos. When I'd brought in my pictures from the motorcycle accident, Kate hadn't even bothered to develop them.

"No," I said to Eric. "I don't think so."

"What do you mean, no?"

"What's the point?" I chased after the fire truck every time I heard a siren. I was happy to follow a police car. But a car crash? "I can get all the details from the police later on."

"Two people died. I want pictures," Eric said.

"Why?" And then I blew it. "You won't run them." I knew I was right, so I kind of smirked. Big mistake.

"I want pictures." Hell hath no fury like an editor smirked at.

So I got in my car, started towards the accident and realized . . . I was about to drive out to an accident to look at dead people. I'd never seen a real live dead body and I didn't really want to. I knew there might be bodies at the plane crash or at the "cabin of death"— but those were big news stories. A car accident was just . . . gross.

I decided to stop by the radio station to see if Steve wanted to drive out with me. He'd invited me to plenty of crime scenes. After waiting patiently for the receptionist to get off the phone with her boyfriend, I discovered Steve had already left to check out the crash. I got back in my car and, just before the turnoff to Horsefly Road, spotted a gas station. The fuel gauge said my tank was precariously close to one-quarter empty, so I pulled in for a fill-up. Then I let the attendant check my oil and top up my wiper fluid. A reporter can never be too careful.

As I turned onto Horsefly Road, I realized I was speeding. Being an upstanding member of the community, I slowed to the speed limit . . . until I saw the ambulance coming from the direction of the accident.

A few minutes later I arrived at the tiny traffic jam. Two dozen cars were stopped along Horsefly Road, waiting for the tow truck to remove the wreckage.

I parked on the shoulder, then walked to the accident scene. The bodies were gone and most of the mess was too. The logging truck had pulled to the side of the road and I took some pictures of scrap metal and a few tires that the police claimed used to be a pickup. Harvey told me the pickup skidded on a patch of ice and ran right into the truck's lane. He said I could get the rest of the details when he got back to the office. He had families to visit first. I let him go and snapped a few more pictures.

I saw Steve's car on the way back to town. I honked and he pulled over. He'd been there before they took the bodies away, but he seemed okay. He'd seen dead people before. I asked what it was like. "A Cariboo specialty," he told me. "A logging truck hits a pickup and what do you get?"

I definitely didn't have an answer for this one.

"Human pâté," Steve chuckled.

I laughed, immediately felt guilty and said, "That's sick." Then I told everyone at work. They laughed, felt guilty about it and said, "That's sick."

I phoned the police, got the full report and whipped off my story. We had the names, the road conditions and the fact that no charges were being laid. The pickup was speeding. On ice. On a logging road. It had slid right into the oncoming lane.

Eric was happy I'd covered the story and he never said a word about the lack of gory photos. As I passed my roll of film to Kate she whispered, "He wouldn't have run them anyway."

※

A few days later I was sitting at my desk trying to make something readable out of an upcoming teen "dry dance." The teens had promised not to drink on-site and, as a publicity stunt, several young girls who looked even less like Madonna than I did, dressed up for a Madonna look-alike contest. So when the phone rang I was delighted to answer it. It was Steve—with actual news. "A truck just rolled down the mountain. Wanna get some pictures? Maybe if we get lucky, it'll explode!"

He picked me up, and I asked how he know about the accident.

"Heard it on the scanner," he said.

"You have a scanner?"

"You don't?"

I felt shame.

"Can't do the job without it," he said. Then . . . "Didn't Sarah tell you the station had a scanner? We've had it for years." If Sarah'd still been my roomie, I would have killed her.

A pickup had indeed rolled off a mountain. The driver was thrown out her door and, outside of a few scrapes and bruises, was unhurt. The police called it a "miracle"—which always makes for a great headline.

We watched the tow-truck driver set up his machine to salvage the pickup. "Dangerous job," said Steve. "If he's not careful, his truck's gonna go right over the cliff too." I moved to take a picture. Then we got the details. The driver had taken a curve too fast and hit an ice patch. I snapped some pictures. We were about to leave when the tow-truck driver called us over.

"You," he said, looking straight at me.

"Me?"

"Yup. Get in the truck."

The truck was resting at the edge of the hill, the same edge the woman's pickup had just rolled down. It was parked on gravel, icy gravel. "I've gotta go down to the pickup. I need someone in the truck."

"Me?" He had to be talking to someone else.

"Get in!"

Before I realized what I was doing, I was in the driver's seat, my hand on the lever that ran the winch, my right foot jammed down against the brake. "When I say go, I want you to raise the lever. And whatever you do," he said, as he climbed down towards the wreck, "don't let up on the brake." That warning may have been the most pointless thing anyone ever told me. If my leg was strong enough, I would have pushed that brake pedal straight through the floor and held the truck in place with my foot, like Fred Flintstone.

Steve snickered. I tried not to look. All that existed in my world was the brake pedal. Steve didn't get to snicker long. He actually stopped quite abruptly when the tow-truck driver told him to get down the hill and help adjust the pulley. Most bystanders would have sensibly declined, but being a reporter, especially in a small town, is like being an extra in a big-budget movie. You go along with pretty much anything, and when you find yourself in an action scene, you hang on for dear life, which is exactly what both of us were doing when the driver shouted for me to turn on his machine. As the winch started spinning, Steve was beneath the raised front end of the wrecked pickup. I could hear gravel spitting out from under the truck's front tires, could feel the truck straining, inching forward and then—

"GOT IT!"

Neither of us moved.

"Thanks, boys. I'll take it from here."

We were frozen in place. I was still terrified to take my foot off the brake and it took all my self-control not to leap out of the truck when I finally did.

As we left the driver to finish his job, we got back in Steve's car and joked about how stupid we were. But that wasn't as stupid as we got.

A few weeks later, when I was driving to work and being careful about the ice, CBC radio reported that a train had derailed near Williams Lake. I pulled over to a payphone just long enough to tell Eric where I was going. Eric sounded concerned. "Haven't you heard? They say it may have been carrying toxic gas."

"I know," I said. "Isn't that cool!" This was way better than any car accident.

"Are you sure you want to—"

"Don't worry, Boss, I've got my camera!" And I hung up.

It didn't matter that it was -18 and I was dressed for a day inside the office—blue jeans, a light sweater and running shoes, not even my nifty new long johns. A train had derailed. This was big-time news.

Steve caught up to me en route to the accident, and we both parked where the railway tracks disappeared into the woods. I pulled on my toque, stuffed my camera and clipboard underneath my leather jacket. Then we started to walk. Fortunately, the snow was only knee-deep because after about 15 minutes of trudging along inside the tracks, we were getting pretty tired. Fortunately, the sweat kept us from focusing on the cold, especially as the sweat iced up all over my beard. But the sweat and the cold and our toques also kept us from noticing the sound of the train racing up behind us. We jumped into a snowbank just a few seconds before the train would have turned us into human pâté. So that was pretty fortunate too.

Covered with snow and frozen sweat, we walked another 20 minutes before we approached the place the small train that barely missed us had stopped.

We looked for someone official to snag quotes from, but no one wanted to talk to "the media." Finally, the only guy there in a suit told me to "phone head office in Vancouver." I had to get something out of him.

"Is it true that the train was carrying toxic gas?"

Silence. But I wasn't going anywhere without an answer. "Was there a toxic gas spill?" He looked at me like I was an alien.

"If there was, we wouldn't be breathing now, would we?" Then he turned around and walked back to the train. Steve and I looked at each other, and it was obvious that thought hadn't occurred to him until now either. Toxic gas could kill reporters too.

I snapped about a half-dozen shots before my shutter froze. Then we trudged back in the opposite direction, this time sticking to the outside of the tracks.

After all, even reporters aren't that stupid twice in a row.

When I got back to the office, Eric told me I was crazy. "It's -18 out there!" So that explained why I could no longer feel my feet. I phoned VIA Rail's head office in Vancouver. The official word: "Nine cars jumped the track, 13 miles north of Williams Lake."

"What was on the train? Anything dangerous?"

"Yes," said the VIA rep. "One of our tankers was carrying sulphur dioxide."

"What's that?"

"We've already got an emergency crew up there. It's highly toxic."

"Uh, how toxic?"

"If it was closer to town we'd have had to evacuate."

So that was probably the dumbest thing I did in Williams Lake. But it wasn't the most dangerous.

# No Left Turns

///

Right after I wrote the slum housing feature, I started getting restless. Everything seemed boring. I even dropped by the high school to see if they had any news. I covered the education beat, but beyond writing up school board meetings, there never seemed to be much to say.

The principal told me his big worry was overcrowding. The school was built for 600 and was handling close to 700. They expected more students next year.

"What this region needs," he said, "is another high school. The board keeps hemming and hawing about how much we need one, but they never do anything about it."

I nodded sympathetically and thought, "Probably because it's too boring."

That night I went for pizza with Kate and scared the locals by ordering beef, mushrooms, feta cheese and pineapple. "The feta's for Greek salads," the waitress told me. We'd had this conversation before.

"It's good on pizzas too," I said. She stared at me like I was crazy, and went to tell the chef about my sacrilegious request.

"I don't know what's wrong," I told Kate.

"You've written your big story," she said. "You put your heart into the slum-housing feature and you're never gonna top it. You're ready to go."

I'd been ready to go since I got there.

And I wasn't sure it was writing the story that burned me out. I think what really bothered me was how little it had accomplished. Maybe I'd seen too many episodes of *Lou Grant*, but I'd really thought my features were going to help people. I thought that if you gave people the facts and told the story properly, you could change the world, or at least a little corner of it.

That's why the story about the bus route to the Elmdale Trailer Court meant so much to me. It wasn't a big deal in the grand scheme of things. I didn't end racial discrimination or bring master criminals to justice, but . . .

It was a slow news day, the kind of day that meant the paper was going to be full of city-council briefs, rewritten press releases and follow-ups to the previous paper's top stories.

There was nothing exciting, nothing urgent, so Abby suggested I drive to the Elmdale Trailer Court. I'd written a short item about it once. The parents living there had complained to the school board because the school bus wouldn't stop there, so their kids had to cross the highway twice a day to get on and off the bus. The board told them nothing could be done, and that was the end of the story. It never occurred to me to follow it up, but Abby suggested it was worth a visit. I didn't believe her, but it sure beat shuffling files, trying to look busy.

So off I went to meet Melissa Hall. She was in her early 20s, and her 7-year-old son, Adrian, had to walk to the bus stop every morning. It made Melissa nervous. That sounded like a typical mom worry to me, certainly not news. But Melissa phoned a few other anxious moms, and 15 minutes later, 6 of us were walking the route that the 17 children who lived in the trailer court walked twice each weekday.

After we left the lot, we reached Highway 97, the major logging route. As we walked along the shoulder, a full logging truck barrelled past us, and the road shuddered. "There are lots of those when school gets out," said Melissa. "The trucks are all going up empty when the kids are walking to the bus in the morning and they're coming back full when the kids get home from school."

We continued our march along the shoulder for about half a mile, until it was time to cross the road.

There was no crosswalk, just a clear stretch of highway far

enough from the hill that you could sort of see what was coming. "The other day a little boy slipped on a patch of ice. A truck was coming," said Melissa, "but he got up in time." There was silence as each mother pictured her child on the highway, imagined a logging truck hitting a patch of ice . . .

As we walked back to the trailers, the mothers shared their horror stories, their nightmares. They told me about the school-board bureaucrat's claim that a left-turn lane would have to be set up and that would take time, money and, worst of all, paperwork.

So I went back to the *Trib* and wrote the mothers' stories in the most impassioned prose I could. Eric ran it on page one. Like I said, it was a slow news day. I also wrote a column for the editorial page about the danger their children faced. I wanted the people who read that column to imagine their child standing on the shoulder of the icy highway next to a speeding logging truck.

The next day I talked to someone at the highways ministry who assured me the bureaucrats were wrong and a special left-turn lane was unnecessary. That ended up on page one too—the morning of the bimonthly school board meeting.

As soon as I walked into the school board offices to cover the meeting, I broke into the biggest grin I'd had during my entire stay in the Cariboo. The place was packed tighter than that proverbial barrel full of hogs people in the Cariboo loved to talk about.

"Hey," a voice behind me said. It was Steve. "I think someone read your story."

An average school board meeting was considered well attended if there were three observers, including me and Steve, but that night the gallery was full, and so was the hallway. The back door was open so everyone could breathe. Steve and I could barely squeeze through to our "media table," and when we got there, all the seats were taken by angry parents. Other parents were sitting on the table. I was happy to stand.

The trustees scowled at me. One managed a grimace and whispered, "I guess we have you to thank for this."

The board quickly declared a new first order of business. "Is there any reason we shouldn't have the school bus stop at the Elmdale Trailer Court?" one trustee asked nervously.

The bureaucrat in charge of bus routes valiantly attempted to explain his position to the angry parents, the angry voters. He explained that a bus driver tried to turn there, but there were so many logging trucks barrelling down the highway, she didn't think it was safe.

So the bus driver didn't think it was safe to turn on the road that the board was making little kids cross twice a day, five times a week? As the crowd started transforming into a mob, one of the trustees averted a lynching by suggesting a vote. Melissa and a few of the other moms stopped to thank me as they filed out. The bus began turning into Elmdale the following Monday. And for one brief moment, I felt like the Lone Ranger.

# *Union Dues*

///

I didn't know it, but the same night I decided not to track down my friend at the *Province* to find out how to start a union, Kate got on her phone. She planned to spend her life in Williams Lake, and she hoped to spend a lot of it at the paper.

Now a group of us were sitting on the couches downstairs at the Women's Centre. Not everyone was from the newsroom. There were a dozen people from the other departments, too. Stu McGuire, a husky dude in his late 40s who looked like he'd been in a few fights, lost as many as he'd won and loved them all, told us about the International Typographical Union. We were too small a paper to even attract the attention of the Newspaper Guild.

The more Stu talked about how brave we were for contacting him, the more everyone shuffled nervously as we realized that just by attending this "informational" meeting we'd already committed ourselves.

This was a small town. Word would get out. Stu didn't do anybody's sense of well-being any good when he warned us, "There will be threats. You might get fired. Or locked out. Things probably won't get violent though."

Violent? I don't think any of us had ever considered the possibility of violence.

"Are all of you willing to stick it out? Is anybody planning to leave?"

I was going to keep my plans a secret, but it didn't seem right. I told him, told everyone, that I was giving notice right after the Christmas holidays. I'd applied for a Canada Council grant and, with or without it, I was going home to Vancouver to produce a satirical show to coincide with Expo 86, Vancouver's world fair. I'd even come up with my title: *Exposé: Sometimes the World's Fair, Sometimes it Ain't.*

And even if I wasn't leaving, I didn't get how a union would help me, since I was the low person on the seniority totem pole. "I'll sign the card and vote "yes," I said, "but other than that I don't want to be involved."

"That's fair," said Stu. "Anyone else planning to leave?"

Everyone else said "no." Then we all signed cards to apply for certification in the International Typographical Union.

Had we thought about the repercussions?

Kate had. After everyone else left, she hung around and we paced the kitchen talking about what the company might try to do to us. We knew this wouldn't be seen as a small movement in the newsroom, or even the *Trib*, but as a threat to Stan's entire chain of small-town papers. Kate figured we might all be fired and replaced by scabs—and these wouldn't be cute cookie scabs either. We talked bravely about walking the picket line. Neither of us expected what happened next.

First the pressmen, who had claimed to be interested in organizing, didn't show up at the next union meeting. Then the women from the back-shop jammed out too. That left five of us: the newsroom.

And that's when things started to get scary.

Because I was a city boy, because I was the outsider and the guy who started the dangerous trend of eating lunch at lunchtime, Stan assumed I was the agitator. So in order to break the union, he decided to break me. One person in management promised me that if the paper went union, I'd be blacklisted from every community paper in Canada. Since I had no overwhelming desire to continue in the community newspaper biz, I thought this was kind of funny. I laughed. That was a mistake. People who saw me laugh thought this guy, who was known for his nasty streak, was going to put me through the wall.

I told Stu what happened. He handed me a page from our paper. The classified ads. One was circled: "We need a few good men who can shoot straight with a .38." Stu said a *Trib* staffer had handed the paper to him and said, "That's the kind of people we have in this town. If I were you, I'd leave. Now."

Stu hadn't gone to the police. "No point. My word against his. And police don't always like union organizers."

I nodded like we were brothers in arms.

Stu told me he'd been threatened before, that he'd dealt with Teamsters in the United States, in the South. If this was supposed to calm me down it didn't work. Good for you, I thought. That's your crazy job. I wanna go home.

"You okay?" he asked.

"Oh yeah," I lied.

I didn't care about a blacklist, but this was insane. I called Barb. She told me to get the hell out of there. That sounded like pretty sane advice. It was time to go.

The next day, the same tough cowboy who'd visited Stu moseyed into my office, stood much too close to me and told me to think hard about what I was doing. "We wouldn't want this to get to the point where a bunch of the boys have to discuss this with you out in the parking lot." There was nothing ambiguous about what he was saying. If we discussed this in the parking lot, I'd be lucky if all I lost in the discussion were my teeth. This time I didn't laugh.

It was like a scene from *Pale Rider*. And what happened after he left the office must have been Clint's fault, because it couldn't have been me talking. I turned to the other people in the newsroom, asked if they'd heard what had just happened. From the looks on their faces I already knew the answer. "Good," I said, "because I'm telling the police." And I knew then—without any trace of doubt—that I couldn't leave until after the vote.

I called Barb and told her I was staying. I didn't tell her why. I didn't know how to explain it. She cried and told me I was an asshole.

But I knew why I couldn't go. Not now. It was just like the movie. I knew somehow that if I left, if I ran away, that it would define who I was. Forever. Even if I never told anyone why I quit, even if no one but these few people from this small town I'd probably never visit again once I left knew the truth, I'd know. I'd know I'd run away.

The next day I visited Staff Sergeant O'Donnell and told him what was said and who'd said it. He asked if I wanted to file a complaint. "No, but this way if anything happens to me, you'll know who to look for." I pictured myself in the parking lot. Face down. I suspect he did too. Although I'd bet I found the image a lot more distressing.

He nodded.

"Thank you, Staff Sergeant O'Donnell," I said.

"Call me Glenn," he said. Then he asked if I was okay.

And I put on a brave face that would have done Clint proud and said, "Yeah, I just thought you should know."

Later, when I was walking home in the dark, I heard footsteps behind me, spun around as fast as I could—swinging my arm like a baseball bat, aiming the flat bone of my forearm—the radius, I think—at the level I expected to find my attacker's throat.

I hope I scared that raccoon as badly as she scared me. I'd read somewhere that using your arm like that and aiming for the throat was a good way to kill someone. I realized if it had been Kate behind me, I could have killed her.

If you'd asked me before I came to Williams Lake whether I could kill someone, I would have said no. I didn't even think I could hurt someone. When my friend Bob spent some time in the army reserve, I told him that if there was ever a war, I'd have to be a conscientious objector because I couldn't imagine killing anyone, for any reason. But when I realized that not only were the anti-union people at the *Trib* not kidding about being willing to hurt me, but the Bajardis were out there too, I started sleeping with a carving knife on my bedside table. Or at least I tried to sleep. I was having nightmares every time I dozed off. And I was dozing off a lot, because I wasn't sleeping.

The window of my room was adjacent to the garage roof. The window didn't lock. It was something I hadn't cared about when I'd moved in. Besides my car I had nothing worth stealing. But suddenly I was acutely aware of how easy it would be to climb into my bedroom.

A few days later, the guy who'd threatened to meet me in the parking lot came up to the office to tell us all how his buddy Ralph almost got shot on the weekend. He was talking to Eric, but he was looking at me.

I asked him why the police hadn't told me about it. "Ralph didn't call 'em."

Apparently Ralph was fooling around with his buddy Mick's wife, Janie. The single bullet ended up in Ralph's wall—a few feet from his head. Janie had just left the house. When my new friend left, I asked the other people in the office why Ralph didn't call the police. Everyone looked at me like I was the crazy person, even Kate. "He was fooling around with the guy's wife."

"But he could have been killed!"

Abby laughed. "Mick's a hunter. He's a great shot. If he wanted to kill Ralph, he would have." This didn't seem strange to anyone. That's just how people settled things around here.

And when I walked by the "sporting goods" shop that afternoon I wondered if, just maybe, I should ignore everything I'd ever believed about guns and buy one. I'd never imagined I could hurt anyone. I hadn't even hit anyone since elementary school. (A bully had attacked me. I'd reflexively hit him back and scored a lucky shot—I knocked him unconscious. At 10 years old I didn't know what unconscious was. I thought I'd killed him. I sat behind a hill in the back of the school and cried. And when he finally found me, I was so happy he was alive that I told him he could do whatever he wanted to me, but I wasn't going to defend myself. I promised myself then that I was never going to hit anyone again.)

But I'd always trusted the system. I always figured that if anything bad ever happened, the police would be there. And now I wasn't convinced that if I called, the police would show up. At least not all that quickly.

It also hit me that if it really was a choice between these people and me, I'd be lying if I didn't admit that I liked me better.

# Death Takes
# the Holidays

%%

It was January 2 at about noon. I left the office
to grab my daily ration of Coke and discovered my store was
closed. So was the store around the corner. And the store down
the block. I returned to the paper and declared that everyone in
town had gone missing.

"They're not missing," said Kate. "They're off for the holiday."

"What holiday?"

"What holiday would logically follow Boxing Day," she asked
and looked at me like I was an ignorant city slicker. I know
Boxing Day is theoretically a holiday, but I think the only people
who still manage to take that day off are Santa and Rudolph.
Even the elves and Mrs. Claus line up at the North Pole mall at 6
a.m. to grab those gatecrasher specials. Before I could come up
with some stupid answer like "New Year's," she hit me with the
correct response: "Wrestling Day." I assumed this was another
Cariboo tall tale created to abuse city slickers, something like
the bear hoop trap or environmentalist duck hunters.

But Kate explained that Wrestling Day was a real honest-to-
Cariboo cowboy holiday created in the 1950s to acknowledge
one of the undisputed facts of life—that on the day after New
Year's, most of the cowboys are wrestling with hangovers. Since
there were only a dozen merchants here back in the '50s, it wasn't
tough to convince them all to take the day off.

I wrote that year's annual tribute to the town's glorious

tradition and discovered Wrestling Day was first proclaimed an official civic holiday in 1959. With the exception of 1977, when city council briefly misplaced its sense of humour and cancelled the grand occasion, it had been celebrated religiously ever since. There were no Wrestling Day TV specials, songs or decorations, but the stores were closed, so were the banks, and all government employees took the holiday.

How do you celebrate Wrestling Day? I got a quote from an old-timer. "Relax. Nurse that hangover. Stay in bed. Visit friends. Don't go shopping. And don't work."

Unless you work for a paper that publishes the next day.

One of the holiday's founders, Syd Western—I am not making that name up—told the *Trib* a few decades earlier the idea of taking the day off "just became a habit." And how could a Wild West town like Williams Lake possibly say no to the idea of a holiday created by a guy named "Western?"

It was the perfect way to start the new year, and as long as no one tried to shoot me, I was looking forward to 1986.

I also scored a great holiday item about the pope endorsing Rick Hansen's Man in Motion Tour.

But just when I was trying to figure out what else to write on a day with no news, I remembered why I didn't want to be a newspaper reporter.

There was a letter in the paper's New Year's issue from Marina Murray. She claimed her husband had died while waiting for open-heart surgery. She blamed the provincial government's economic program—dubbed "restraint" during the previous election campaign—for her husband's death. I never read letters to the editor. I should have read this one. Everybody else had.

"My husband, Carson, died today. He need not have died, at least not without a fighting chance, which was denied him because of restraints by our government. He needed open-heart surgery. But the doctors at Vancouver General Hospital had to send him home, to be recalled the first week in January, because one of the three operating rooms was shut down due to restraints, as well as at least one floor because they could not afford the staff. He died at our home in Williams Lake on Dec. 22, on the kitchen floor."

The letter ended: "Merry Christmas Premier Bennett."

Marina had obviously sent her letter to a few papers, because Eric got a call about it from the *Province*. They were flying a reporter out and wanted Eric to take pictures.

"I know news when it kicks me in the teeth," said Eric.

"You want me to interview the . . . " I hesitated. I don't think I'd ever said the word before. "Widow?"

"It's our town and we're not going to let the *Province* beat us to the story."

"Can Abby write it?"

Eric flashed a you-gotta-be-kidding smile. "This'll be great. Maybe if you get to her fast enough you can resell it to the *Province* yourself." Ever since the *Sun* made my cheque out to Neil Leisen-Young, I'd been stringing for the *Province*. All they wanted were paragraph-long tales of weird incidents or violent death. They tossed them into a section called "BC Briefs," where they reported the weirdest and/or most gruesome events taking place outside of Vancouver and Victoria, and they sent me cheques for $30 an item. If I wasn't going to be paid well, I may as well work for someone who didn't want me to do any work.

I knew I could sell the story. This one was big enough that they might even let me write it properly, pay me properly. I didn't care. "Let Abby do this. Please."

"Abby's busy," said Eric. "It's a gift. This one's gonna be big."

Kate was told to join me. She'd done this type of thing before. And we needed pictures—this was "human interest"—especially if the widow was pretty.

I didn't want to go. Kate offered to drive. She had a pickup. With chains. "It's a great story," she said.

"I wish Abby would do it."

Kate looked surprised. "You've covered everything else. What's the big deal?"

"It's not news," I said.

"The guy dies on the waiting list. Of course it's news. It's huge."

"But . . ." I wasn't sure how to explain it. I had no problem with the idea that murders and plane crashes are news. I'd just never liked the idea of invading the private traumas of a private person, and even if this woman was anxious to tell her story, it still felt wrong. And that's really all I could say. "It feels wrong."

Kate was philosophical. "If you don't do it, somebody else will. And they probably won't have your conscience."

I pictured Steve getting the widow to cry on the radio.

Kate pulled her pickup into the gravel driveway of what looked like a model home. A wood A-frame that was so new you could practically smell the sawdust. By the time Kate parked the car, the door was already open and Marina was on the porch, waiting for us. If you'd wanted to design the perfect grieving widow for a story about a senseless death, it would have been hard to do better. She was 31, blonde and intense to the point of intimidating. She'd done her crying and now she wanted to talk.

Her children were staying with relatives in Kamloops. She was alone in the kitchen with her polished oak cupboards and her husband's ghost. She ushered us to the wooden kitchen table. "Carson made this," she said. "He made this too." She gestured to indicate what I assumed were the cabinets and cupboards. Kate knew better.

"He built the house?"

Marina nodded.

"Beautiful," said Kate. I still hadn't said anything but "hi." I wasn't sure what else to say. Then I said yes to the offer of a cup of tea and managed to ask the only question I had to. "What happened?"

"He was on the waiting list for open-heart surgery. Cariboo Memorial had flown him to Vancouver by helicopter. His doctor discovered a congenital defect that had almost completely clogged a heart valve. The doctor said he needed surgery."

"But they flew him back?"

"The hospital didn't have the beds," she said. "He was flown home with a bottle of nitroglycerine tablets in his coat pocket and an order to return right after the holidays. Every movement he made was a strain," Marina explained. "He could barely walk to the bathroom without stopping to catch his breath."

He was sent home December 20. He made it through two more days. Marina deposited our tea on the table, then crossed to the refrigerator for the cream. I asked how he died.

"Carson was sitting right there"—she pointed to me—"where you are now. And we were drinking tea. He just keeled over."

A chill shot down my spine. I know it's a cliché, but my spine didn't. Even thinking about it now and the matter-of-fact way she said it, and the pained look in her eyes as she seemed to watch him die again, his ghost superimposed over my body, I still remember the shudder. I wanted to change seats, but knew it would be cruel. I wanted to leave. She needed friends with her, family, not a reporter and a photographer.

After tea, she offered to take us on a tour of the house. I had to stop myself from jumping out of the chair. They'd finished their home that summer, and it was the type of idyllic country home that city folks dream of moving to when they retire.

I took notes. Kate asked if there were any photos of Carson we could borrow. It was classic old-school reporting. They used to call it "picture chasing"—getting photos of victims, and getting them before the *Province* could.

Marina took us upstairs to the empty bedroom and brought out a photo album. Kate talked about architecture and house design while Marina flipped through the album, carefully thumbing her way past vacation snapshots of a happy family on the beach. Kate asked for a photo of a young, handsome, very healthy-looking man who was hang-gliding against the backdrop of a clear blue sky. Then she borrowed another photo that showed him tanned and surfing.

Marina was very polite, very controlled. She never raised her voice, never came close to tears, even when she told me point-blank, "Premier Bennett murdered my husband." It was the type of quote reporters live for. I almost forgot to write it down.

She'd made sense of a senseless death, and there was no

time for grief until she had done all she could to avenge herself against her husband's killer.

The story was irresistible, and after the *Province* put it on their front page, everybody wanted it—the newspapers, the TV news, the radio talk shows. I saw her on TV a few times and never saw her cry. That was for later, I suspect, after she'd done all she could. A government member of the legislature got so upset with all the press Marina was getting that he claimed she was being used by the NDP, the official opposition.

As for my story in the *Trib*, Eric topped it with a banner head-line: "Widow Blames Restraint for Death."

My lead: "Surgery Urgent."

"That was the message a doctor scrawled next to a diagram of Carson Murray's heart before placing him on Vancouver General Hospital's waiting list for open heart surgery and send-ing him home."

Beside my story was Kate's picture of the widow holding up the doctor's sketch of her husband's defective heart.

I followed the story the next issue with an interview with a Vancouver cardiologist who agreed with Marina that her husband's true cause of death was lack of hospital funding. A woman from Horsefly wrote in to cancel her subscription to the *Trib*. She said the way I covered the story was "sensational" and "offensive."

A few days earlier, there had been an apparently healthy 40-year-old man with a young wife and three children. Now he was dead. The woman from Horsefly was right. The story was sensational and hopefully, at least a little offensive. I couldn't see any other way to tell it.

But I never wanted to write anything like it again.

# *Blizzard Hits Newsroom*

A battle was brewing in Anahim Lake, and Stan wanted me to cover it. It sounded like a great story. The business people and the folks who lived off the land were at war over a proposed road.

The businessmen said the road would mean—surprise—more business. The tour guides and back-to-the-landers said it would destroy the wilderness and ruin their lifestyles. Somebody started setting fires to get their point across. The businessmen said it was the back-to-the-landers. They said the businessmen were trying to frame them.

It was the dead of winter, a phrase that doesn't mean much unless you're talking -40, with a wind chill that can kill you. Actually, that day it was just a few degrees below zero, and that was even scarier, because it was starting to snow. Stan was in one of his journalist moods. After he told me to go to Anahim, he instructed me to "get both sides of the story" and "get your facts straight." There was only one problem with Stan's plan, and it had nothing to do with his use of journalistic homilies. The problem was I didn't want to go. It wasn't just that I suspected he was sending me off to do a hatchet job on the anti-road group for the benefit of his business buddies. It wasn't even that I felt it would be impossible to get such a close-knit community to give an honest account of what was going on in the few days I'd have with them. I just didn't want to go. It was the Thursday before a long weekend and the end of an incredibly long week. If I could get through the snow, I was driving to Vancouver.

"It's a long weekend."

Stan looked completely baffled. "There's a town meeting Saturday night. Everyone will be there." I didn't care. I had to find a way out of this. "If I'm going to spend three days covering this story I want to make sure I still get three days off later on." Eric was in shock. I couldn't believe I was saying this either. Nobody asked Stan for days off, that was almost as dangerous as mentioning the forbidden word, "overtime."

"Okay," said Stan. I think I heard Eric sigh. "So when do I get the time off?" Eric glared at me the way a parent glares when their child asks a visiting rich aunt why she's fat. Rick and Liz edged closer to watch the fireworks.

Nobody ever asked Stan for anything. "Whenever," said Stan, perfectly calmly, "just so long as you give us a bit of advance warning. Now, when you're up there—"

"What about money?" Once more Stan was puzzled. Eric was mortified. "Money" was an even scarier word than overtime. "To be honest, I'm kind of broke right now." Which was true. I could hardly afford gas, never mind food and a hotel room. I didn't have a credit card, except one for a gas station chain that didn't exist in the Cariboo. "There's no way I can afford to stay up there without some kind of advance."

By this time, the entire staff was lurking near the door to watch Stan fire me. There are two possible explanations for what happened next. One is that the legend was just that, and Stan was actually a reasonable man who would treat people fairly if they'd only get up the courage to openly explain what they wanted and why. The other possibility, which I kind of prefer, is that Stan was so taken by my courage, gall or naïveté that he was moved to do the unthinkable. He offered me a $300 advance against expenses. "Just make sure you keep all your receipts."

I thought Eric might die on the spot, and the rest of the staff looked ready to pass out when I stopped Stan from leaving with one more question.

"I've only got one more problem. I don't know if my car is going to be able to make it through serious snow."

I was pretty sure I'd gone too far. I was kind of hoping I had.

"You can borrow my Jeep," said Stan. "It's four-wheel drive and it can handle just about anything."

After being offered three days of flexible vacation time, a $300 advance and use of Stan's Jeep, it was time to shut up and listen to my assignment—which was just as well because if I'd come up with any more demands, I don't think Eric's heart could have handled the strain. The only catch was that I had to go to Anahim Lake and, as Kate announced, the radio was calling for a blizzard. Abby made me promise to pack a shovel, a candle, matches and flares. The most useful things I'd ever kept in my car was extra ketchup in case the person at the drive-through forgot it in my order.

"The shovel is for digging out your tires. The candle is to keep you warm if you're stuck."

"And the flares?"

"I'll loan you flares," she said.

"What are they for?"

"In case you need them," she said. "These aren't very busy roads."

I traded car keys with Stan and drove his Jeep to the Overlander. We'd been invited to do one more performance of *The Apollo* that night as a fundraiser, so I'd leave for Anahim the next morning. After the show, I got in the Jeep that could handle anything and flicked the switch to turn on the four-wheel drive. The snow was falling so heavily I wouldn't have even tried to leave the parking lot with my car. The Overlander was at the top of a steep hill that led straight down to the main highway. But this was a Jeep. A new Jeep. With power everything. I went to the exit, started down slowly, pumping the brakes. And pumping. And pumping.

As I started picking up speed en route to the highway I pumped those brakes some more and I discovered that even perfect brakes on a new four-wheel-drive Jeep can't handle a sheet of fresh ice on a steep hill.

It's amazing how many things can flash through your head in the few seconds it takes a runaway Jeep to speed downhill towards a major logging highway. I considered undoing my safety belt, opening the door and jumping out. I thought of swerving or pulling the emergency brake and intentionally wiping out on the hill to avoid the possibility of becoming a hood ornament on a logging truck.

But the plan that won was jamming my hands against the horn to warn whoever was below and starting to pray as the Jeep flew like a bobsled towards Highway 97. And as I prayed, I remembered Steve's joke about human pâté. I didn't laugh.

I guess the prayer worked, because no one else was stupid enough to be driving that night. Even other people with four-wheel-drive Jeeps that could handle anything knew better than to be cruising Highway 97 in a blizzard. The Jeep finally stopped when the front tires hit the curb of a traffic island and for some reason—I'm not ruling out the prayer—the Jeep didn't flip.

I was so shaken that I drove about a block to the nearest pay phone, called Abby—since she was the one who'd told me not to drive and the one who knew about Jeeps—and started crying. She told me to drive to her house. And that's where I went. Very slowly. As soon as I walked in, she and her husband told me how crazy I was to go down that hill in that weather. They made me a cup of tea and we sat, watched some TV and I played with their cat, Scooter, before they sent me to spend the night in their spare bedroom. They weren't letting me drive anywhere else.

I'd been out cold for about an hour before I felt a thump on my bed. I sat bolt upright and screamed. And screamed. And screamed. It was Scooter.

Anyone who thinks putting a cat in a horror movie like *Alien* just to score a cheap jolt is a cheat has never been jumped on by a cat a few hours after they thought they were going to die.

I woke up the next morning to Abby shouting, "He's not going to Anahim!" I could imagine Stan at the other end of the line, smoke coming from his ears. I didn't hear what he said, but I heard her response. "Because he's a stupid city boy who can't drive in the snow and last night he almost flipped your Jeep!" I'd hardly had time to wipe the sleep from my eyes before Stan arrived to swap cars. To be honest, sliding helplessly towards a major highway in a runaway Jeep was not part of my original bargaining plan, but I never did get to Anahim Lake.

※

Stan kept trying to talk us out of unionizing.

He would come upstairs and tell us how he'd never imagined how unhappy we were, how he would be glad to work things out if only we got rid of the union. "A union will only complicate things."

And some of what he said made sense to me. Except every time I almost came around to his way of thinking, I remembered the threats and I knew that if I changed my mind now, I'd never believe it was logic that swayed me. Even if everyone else did.

Then I got a call from an editor at another community paper. The editor said he really liked my writing. He wanted me right away. He'd pay me $200 a month more than the *Trib*. I passed.

In a startling coincidence, I was offered another job a week later—at an even better paper on Vancouver Island—for even more money. It was a hell of an offer . . . if I'd wanted a career in community news.

The night before the certification vote, I spent an hour interrupting a relatively sane conversation between Liz and "one of them." I responded to every anti-union argument as well as I could.

To be fair, the propaganda was flying at us from both sides. There were pep talks, epic conversations and all sorts of generic "unions are great" letters arriving in the mail. With time running out, the company made a final peace offer. "We can't give you a contract or sign anything now, but if you vote 'no' we'll give you . . . " And the offer was tempting, really tempting. More money. Overtime. Job security. Everything everyone had hoped the union could get us.

Kate and I spent the night before the vote pacing her kitchen. She must have smoked a pack of cigarettes and gone through a tub of coffee. I'd gone through at least as much Coke.

She'd made the call. She couldn't back out.

They'd threatened me. I couldn't back out.

But both of us figured anything could happen with Liz and Abby and Rick, and we braced for the possibility that we might lose the vote three to two. We'd both be fired. She'd be unemployed and unemployable. And I'd be heading home. And as much as I wanted to leave, that wasn't how I wanted to go.

We all went to lunch the day before the vote. It was a Chinese food buffet—we couldn't risk everyone overhearing us at the Dog 'n' Suds. The five of us sat around the Lazy Susan picking at the chow mein and chicken balls and trying not to look scared. The arguments flew a lot faster than the chopsticks. Kate tried to convince everyone to stick with the union, but Rick, Liz and Abby didn't seem sold.

Then I launched into my best Clarence Darrow routine. "If we make any deals now it would be the equivalent of a shotgun wedding. The company will be able to say they signed under duress, that we blackmailed them. Suddenly, we'll be the bad guys. I don't know about any of you, and to be honest I don't care any more, these people threatened me. And now you want to trust them because they're running scared? I don't care if I'm the only one who votes 'yes,' but I refuse to look like I've been threatened into changing my vote."

So much for not getting involved.

I remember the worst part. The worst part was wondering, even as I tried to convince my friends to vote "yes," if I was doing the right thing. Maybe management was right and the union wouldn't care about us once we signed. After all, why should an international organization worry about five people in a small town in the interior of BC? They'd been hoping to unionize the entire paper and then the chain and then the whole community paper world, and all they had were a handful of reluctant rebels. Even as I let loose with my rhetoric I felt sick at the thought that maybe, just maybe, this was all a huge mistake.

It was a secret ballot, but when the votes were counted, the secret was out. The final score was ITU: 5—*Tribune*: 0.

Eric was technically management, but he had the same problems we did, so his position was sympathetic, but officially neutral. He wasn't interested in sparking a fight with Stan, but he knew that any union drive was news. So, at Eric's request, my story explaining that we'd gone union was probably the blandest piece I'd ever written. It blamed the company for nothing, said "we had some problems" and that we felt belonging to a union would help us deal with them.

The column was dummied and ready to go when Stan tore it from the page. I was told that if we printed "our side," the company would have to print a story explaining "their side." I said this was hardly a pro-union statement and if the company wrote anything then I could certainly rewrite my column to explain our position more thoroughly. Eric decided against covering the story.

That night, while I was driving home from work, I spotted a black pit in the alley. I didn't know how it got there, but I knew if I didn't stop in time, I was dead. I slammed on the brakes, skidded and spun out on the ice. When I finally stopped I saw . . .

The same alley that had always been there. No pit. And instead of feeling calmer, I felt like my heart was trying to jump out of my chest. I took a deep breath and remembered I only had two more weeks. Just two more weeks before I gave notice and went home.

Three days later Liz announced she was quitting. The stress was too much for her. She'd taken a job at a paper on Vancouver Island (coincidentally, it was the same one that had tried to hire me). Eric took a new job at another paper in the chain too. He wasn't fired, but Stan couldn't have been thrilled that his staff went union.

Kate called me into her darkroom. "You're really giving notice too, aren't you?"

"Yeah," I said.

She looked too exhausted to cry. "I can't believe it. We've been unionized a week, and half the staff's gonna be gone by February."

"Yeah," I said. "I'm sorry." I reminded her I'd been planning this since before the union had shown up. I'd agreed to stay for the vote but, after that, I was getting out of Dodge. It was my plan. It had always been my plan.

"I know," she said. "I know."

And I knew I couldn't give notice yet.

# "Canada's Ozarks"

I couldn't help laughing.

Fortunately nobody saw. Nobody except Steve, and he was laughing too and fighting desperately to keep quiet. I dug my fingernails deep into the palms of my hands, finally got my breathing under control, then looked at Steve and we both started giggling again. Then we snuck out of the courtroom as discreetly as possible. People aren't supposed to laugh in court, especially during sexual abuse trials.

The facts of the case were typically horrific. The accused was a stepfather. (In court the word "stepfather" seemed to be synonymous with "molester.") The kids were a 14-year-old girl and a 9-year-old boy. The kinks included the general sexual repertoire and a strip of car tire the bastard used to whip the kids with when he decided they'd been "bad." Not all that funny, I know.

Even for Williams Lake, this month's cases were bizarre. It was as if all the lawyers and judges had gone for drinks and agreed to get all the sick stuff over with at once. The County Court circuit judge was in town and commandeered a meeting room, so there were three trials running simultaneously in a building with only two courtrooms, and all of the trials were for sex crimes.

Steve and I agreed to share notes, because it was the only way we could cover every story—and that week they were all big enough to qualify as news. Abby took over the case of a man charged with kidnapping and sexually assaulting a Mohawk clerk who'd worked at the gas station before Tina started.

Steve took the stepfather with the tire fetish. I got the main courtroom as Judge Turner listened to the story of a foster parent who had allegedly molested one of his juvenile charges. "A precocious girl," the defence lawyer told me privately. "Be careful with this one." He believed, or at least wanted me to believe, that the girl's accusations were a calculated attack on an authority figure with no basis in reality. Not an impossibility with a streetwise kid.

I hoped he was right. The accused, Peter Allan Evans had been a foster parent for years. Dozens, maybe hundreds, of children had filtered through his house.

It was only "oral" sex she was accusing him of. There were no special kinks, no injuries, and she said it only happened once. It was only news because he was a foster parent. If it was true.

In my vast nine months of experience as a court reporter, I'd already learned not to trust verdicts. It seemed to me that a trial was a sophisticated game, and the better lawyer—whoever casts the most doubts—wins. That doesn't mean the bad guys don't go to jail, just that almost as many of them seemed to go home or weren't sent away long enough. So even though all I could write about was what everyone said, I trusted my response to the people in the box, the people on the witness stand. And when the girl took the stand, she looked scared and ashamed. I'd been in enough plays to know that if she was acting, she was better than anybody I'd ever seen take home an award.

She didn't break down in tears, she wasn't tabloid sensational, but a foster parent on trial for abuse was a damn good story. Especially after the judge pronounced him guilty.

I'd covered at least two dozen sexual assault cases, and they no longer made me lose my appetite. When all the trials broke for lunch, Steve and I went for Coney burgers and shared notes. Abby had left the courthouse after her trial ended with a guilty verdict and a six-year sentence for the accused. "They're all inbred out there in the Chilcotin," said Steve.

I laughed, but I didn't feel shame. I finished my Coney fries. And I thought, just maybe, I was a better person six months earlier when this sort of story would have made me sick for a week.

When we got back to court Steve and I both went to the down-stairs courtroom—the one with the stepfather, the 14 year-old girl, the 9-year-old boy and the nocturnal visits when Mama was sleeping, or pretending to sleep.

Mama told the court her children were lying, that her hus-band was a good, honest, hard-working man. She sounded like she was reciting the lyrics to a country song—and not even a clever one. Maybe she was. Mama figured the social worker had put her kids up to all this. She figured there was some sort of conspiracy to break up her happy family, and the social worker and the schoolteachers and the doctor and the police were all in on it. That's what she said. And she glared at the judge like he was in on it too.

The social worker had gone to visit the farm after getting a call from the doctor, who got a call from the teacher. The kids attended school in Anahim, and the teacher noticed they were coming to class with bruises, more bruises than kids ought to have. The doctor agreed. "They're all in on it," Mama said. And now she was glaring at the Crown attorney.

So the social worker went to the ranch. She talked to Mama and she talked to the stepdad and she talked to the 14-year-old girl and she talked to the nine-year-old boy, and then she talked to the police. "And what happened then?" asked the Crown.

"Then I took the children from their parents' home and I placed them in a foster home, in the custody of Mr. Peter Allan Evans."

And that's when I started to laugh.

# Indians
# and Cowboys

///

Even though I'd agreed to stay a bit longer, I knew I was leaving soon, so I sat down with Kate one night to discuss the stories I should try to tell before I left. "Who would you most like to write about?" she asked. She knew the answer before she'd asked the question.

The black silk robes of civilized justice with a pair of fancy leather cowboy boots beneath them struck me as the perfect symbol of the Cariboo and the perfect story. I decided to pitch a profile to a national magazine. Freelance.

One afternoon after court was out for the day, I asked the judge if we could talk. He invited me into his office. I told him my idea for a profile, and his response was: "How dare you?"

I didn't know what to say. How dare I what?

Then he started in about my "sensationalized" reporting, and I wasn't sure what hit me. That's when he mentioned some letters to the editor. I really had to start reading those things. The letters were about an attempted murder case I'd covered a few weeks earlier.

A woman named Katie Ross and her son were thrown out of the hotel bar in Horsefly. They were drunk, and once they were outside, Katie started throwing pieces of garbage, including some small wooden boards, at the hotel wall.

The owner, Mike Tandy, picked up the boards and started throwing them back at her. The pair got into a shouting match.

Katie's son, Roland, took the boards from her and tried to lead her away, but Tandy wasn't done fighting. Instead of calling the police, whose office was across the street, Tandy started hurling beer bottles at Katie and Roland.

Katie and Roland left for the general store. A few minutes later Tandy found them. Tandy claimed Katie tossed a five-gallon garbage pail at him (something Judge Turner didn't believe the small woman had done). Judge Turner believed Tandy followed Katie outside and pushed her to the ground.

Roland tackled Tandy to get him off his mom. Someone opened the store doors, and Roland and Tandy fell inside. Tandy landed on top. That's when Katie pulled a knife. She stabbed Tandy. Twice. He almost died. That's why Katie Ross was only charged with attempted murder.

"She had a pocket knife on her person," Judge Turner said in his verdict. "In my experience every Chilcotin Indian woman does. Such knives have many uses in the Chilcotin. Sometimes, unfortunately, they are used in ways which cause injury to other persons. Sometimes that use is offensive, on other occasions the use is defensive."

The Crown felt the use was most certainly "offensive." Crown counsel Kevin Holland argued that Katie Ross wasn't in any danger, because Tandy was attacking her son. He felt the assault on Katie had ended, so she had no claim to self-defence.

Judge Turner disagreed. "In my opinion this submission is too sophisticated—these events all happened quickly. And I believe that a reasonable person could easily have viewed the interaction between Roland Ross and Mike Tandy as a mere interlude in Tandy's outrageous assault on Katie Ross."

What made the trial so controversial is that Tandy was White. Ross was Native.

I missed the case, but caught the verdict—which sparked the controversy of the year.

Judge Turner declared that Tandy had every right to evict people from his bar, but noted he had a reputation for taking great pleasure in doing so, especially when they were Native. Tandy kept a sprayer filled with homemade mace, a mix of ammonia and pepper spray, behind his bar. Everyone in town knew he was happy to use it on disorderly Native patrons. He also kept a club behind the bar and apparently liked to use that too. He wouldn't just ask unruly Native patrons to leave, said Judge Turner, he'd throw them out and, if he had the chance, hurt them.

Judge Turner said Katie Ross had every reason to believe that when Tandy followed her out of the bar, she was in physical danger. "Therefore, she had every right to draw the knife—in self-defence . . . In my opinion it was most unwise of Katie Ross to stab Mike Tandy, but that, of course, is not the issue."

As Judge Turner delivered his verdict, Holland's ears started to leak steam like an angry Elmer Fudd in a classic Looney Tune. He was going to appeal. Immediately. Tandy's friends and family were livid, and so were many of the White folks throughout the Cariboo. It wasn't just the rednecks talking about the verdict. Everyone who knew Tandy, and almost everyone in town seemed to, thought Judge Turner had lost it.

I thought Judge Turner's verdict was intelligent, compassionate and explosive. That's why I tried to print his reasons for judgment in as close to their entirety as possible. I even got the judge to give me a photocopy of his ruling, so I wouldn't have to rely on my shorthand to get this one right. In my story I tried to explain what had happened, and my sympathies were completely with the judge and Katie Ross.

But the letters to the editor about the case called for everything short of lynching Judge Turner, and I wouldn't be surprised if that's just because Eric tossed the lynching letters.

People accused Turner of putting the victim on trial. They said that if Katie was White, she would have gone to jail. One writer demanded an investigation into Turner's behaviour. Others simply demanded he be removed from the bench. The scene was straight out of *To Kill a Mockingbird*.

The letters quoted the verdict out of context. Letters to the editor do stuff like that all the time. It's why I don't read them. When someone writes an editorial or a column, they have to get their facts straight. I've never heard of anyone fact-checking a letter to the editor, especially at a community paper.

And I guess when I stepped into his office, I gave Judge Turner the first chance he'd had to vent his feelings about those letters. Our "conversation" may have lasted only five minutes, but it felt like he went at me for hours.

The next day I visited Lyle Norton, the public defender. He said Judge Turner was frustrated because judges weren't allowed to publicly reply to such things. Eventually Judge Turner wrote a letter to the newspaper, but not for publication. He was generous towards me, saying it was probably the editor's fault that my story was incorrect. But my story wasn't incorrect, and Eric had barely touched it. Judge Turner's letter made me as angry as the letters to the editor had made him. I banged out a two-page response on my computer. I took all his points and refuted them, giving my own evidence.

I clipped a copy of the original article and used a yellow highlighter to show that I had indeed included the information he'd accused me of omitting. And I concluded by saying that if he still felt the tone of my work was sensational then I was to blame, not my editor. It said everything I wanted to say and, I hoped, would regain Judge Turner's respect. Maybe I'd even get to do that story on him after all—the story of the Cariboo judge who sentenced you according to your crime and not your skin colour.

I brought the letter with me to the next trial I covered—a sexual abuse case. An absent-minded attorney started complaining loudly that I should be evicted from the court because of my "irresponsible radio broadcast." Judge Turner smiled at me, then told the sputtering attorney that not only did I write for the newspaper, but I was certainly not irresponsible.

That night I read over my well-reasoned response to Judge Turner's accusations. I realized my letter was at least as angry as his had been, and I tossed it out. I wish I'd rewritten it instead, if only to tell him that when he dismissed the charges against Katie Ross, I thought he did a brave a thing and I was honoured to be there to report it.

# *Bombs Away*

*///*

**A**nd now, here I was, back in Judge Turner's courtroom, stuck between an armed RCMP officer and a suicidal/homicidal lunatic.

I stared at Constable Ron's note. "If we both get out of here alive." And as it sunk in that he thought I might be right, that Fraser might have a bomb strapped to his chest, I scrawled my reply. "Can't you just shoot him or something?"

He didn't respond, just kept his eyes on Fraser.

I contemplated the bulge under Fraser's sweater, wondering if I was going to be hit by shrapnel, blood or body parts.

I was scared. I was fascinated. Maybe I was crazy. But most of all, I was connected. Because I was there, I was a part of it. If Constable Ron told me to go for help, I would have gone. But I was part of Constable Ron's cover. And if I got up, Fraser might wonder if something was going on. He might panic. I knew I could make it to the door if I wanted to. And I definitely wanted to. But somehow I knew, or at least believed, that if I left that courtroom, whatever happened next would be my fault.

Sheriffs Tweedledum and Tweedledee glanced over at Constable Ron, obviously hoping he'd do something. They certainly weren't going to. A few weeks earlier they'd lost a prisoner while walking him across the street to the police station. The prisoner had decided to run, and even though he was handcuffed, they were too out of shape to keep up with him.

The usually abrasive Holland was so polite it was funny. It was only the possibility that Fraser might kill Holland that kept me from laughing.

The stenographer was trying hard not to look up from her machine, because every time she did her eyes gave away how scared she was.

Judge Turner was the only person besides Fraser who didn't seem the least bit flustered. And that was scary too.

Because the only other player, the man who stood accused of a wide variety of physical and sexual assault charges, appeared completely at ease. Or, as I kept thinking, ready to die.

At first I thought Judge Turner was just playing it cool, setting the tone. It wasn't until he announced it was time for the first witness that it occurred to me he might not have noticed the ominous bulge in Fraser's sweater.

Holland's response was slow, deliberate. "The first witness is the defendant's ex-wife, Your Honour."

I scrawled another note to Constable Ron. "What the hell is he doing???"

"That's fine," said Judge Turner.

Holland repeated his statement, glancing over at Fraser's sweater. Judge Turner barely looked up. "Bring her in."

Everybody in the courtroom—okay, everybody except Judge Turner and Fraser—looked stunned. My police pal was tensing. The stenographer looked ready to bolt from the room. The sheriffs seemed set to race her to the door.

Holland almost choked on the words as he spat out, "I really don't think that's a good idea, Your Honour."

Fraser practically growled. "Why not?"

Holland tried not to look at Fraser. Or his sweater.

"Yes, why not?" asked Judge Turner.

"Because," Holland stumbled as he fished for an answer, "it's, uh, almost lunchtime. I really think we ought to take a break for lunch."

"But it's only 11:15."

Holland looked and sounded like a bad ventriloquist as his words slowly made their way out from behind gritted teeth. "I really think we ought to break for lunch. NOW."

Fraser glared at Holland. Holland tried not to notice. Judge Turner looked out at them both before delivering his verdict.

I'll never know what Judge Quentin Turner was thinking while everyone else was convinced we were going to be blown to bits by a crazy man. But I do know that when he said, "Let's break for lunch," everyone in that room besides Judge Turner and Fraser was thinking, "Thank God."

Before Fraser had time to object—or explode—Judge Turner vanished through his chamber door and the stenographer whizzed past me to the exit. Constable Ron and I stepped outside the courtroom too, and I finally had the chance to ask the question that was making me crazy. "Why didn't you do anything in there?"

"I'm not allowed to."

"But you're the police!"

"Not in the courtroom. That's the sheriffs' jurisdiction. I can't touch him without the possibility of a mistrial. We have to wait till he leaves the building."

I wasn't going to wait. I had two thoughts. One, I didn't want to blow up. And two, as soon as the police disarmed this thing, this was going to be a great story—my best ever. I raced to the paper to tell everyone.

Everyone looked at me like I should switch to the community beat and start covering flower shows.

"It's probably just a pacemaker," said Kate.

I found myself growling like Holland. "It was not a pacemaker."

"Well, it sure as hell wasn't a bomb," said Rick. Rick had stepped in as editor while we were waiting for Eric's replacement to arrive. "Do you think someone could get a bomb past court security?" He looked at me like I was an idiot.

"What court security?"

Abby cheerfully suggested it was a figment of my imagination. "Maybe you're working too hard."

I whipped off my weather report, some police briefs and a story on the verdict in another sexual assault case. I was in such a rush to get back to court that my lead read, "A Williams Lake man has been sentenced to six years in jail for buggering his 12-year-old son." The man was convicted of buggery, so I suppose it was technically accurate. Eric would have caught it—and I'm sure Rick did too—but he was so nervous about tinkering with my court stories and potentially upsetting a judge that the line slid into the paper unedited and onto the front page. I suspect it probably shocked even more people than the graveyard shit—but nobody laughed about it, except maybe Steve.

After buggering up the buggery story, I stormed out of the office like a mad scientist, vowing to show them all. "So you think it was just my imagination? We'll see." And we did.

On my way back to court, I drove right past . . . Fraser. I couldn't believe it. He was on the street—alone—and the bulge was still there. Maybe it was a pacemaker. Maybe I was an idiot. Even worse, I was going to have to admit to everyone back in the newsroom that I was wrong.

I went back to the press box and waited for the trial to restart. A few minutes later Constable Ron came in and sat down next to me. "I'm still a reporter," he said. Obviously, he'd decided not to blow his cover by disarming our friend. Then Fraser entered the courtroom. The bulge was gone.

"What was it?" I whispered.

"We don't know yet," Constable Ron whispered back. "The bomb squad is flying up from Vancouver to find out. Fraser's large backpack was gone too. "They're keeping it downstairs," said Constable Ron. That sounded good to me.

Judge Turner re-entered. Holland opened by saying he wanted to discuss placing Fraser in police custody because right now Fraser was on his own recognizance, which was why he could walk around unescorted. Judge Turner wanted to start the trial. The Crown counsel was adamant, and he'd used up a year's worth of polite that morning.

Judge Turner ignored Holland's tone, repeated that he wanted to start the trial and that the other local judge could deal with any custody questions after he got back from Alexis Creek.

Judge Turner said he didn't want to hear anything that could prejudice the case. He didn't want to risk a mistrial.

Holland looked ready to spontaneously combust.

The judge wanted to call the first witness.

That's when Fraser interrupted. "The police took something away from me over the lunch break and I want it back."

Judge Turner looked at Holland. "I assume this had something to do with the custody issue?"

"Yes, Your Honour." I was amazed at how Holland was able to make the word "honour" sound so much like "asshole."

Fraser ignored the exchange. "The police took something that belongs to me and I want it back."

And that's when the police marched through the double doors.

Staff Sergeant O'Donnell, Swanson and two other officers turned towards the public gallery at the back. The fourth officer, Harvey, stood in front of the gallery for a moment near the centre of the courtroom with "something" cradled in his hands. His arms were fully extended as he held a bizarre metal contraption like it was a sleeping cobra.

"It's my meditation device," said Fraser. "It's part of my belief, my religion."

Holland looked like he'd been slapped. The word "religion" had, well, religious significance in a courtroom. "I'm not quite sure what it is, but I know what it isn't," said Holland. "And it isn't a religious icon." It was clear from the way Holland stressed the term that if the device was deemed a "religious icon," Fraser would be allowed to keep it.

"It's my power device," said Fraser. "I must be able to remain in contact with it in order to be able to draw upon it in my time of need."

Connected or not, if Fraser got his hands on that thing again I was going right out the door.

"I have used it twice this morning," said Fraser. "Many times I've gone to it to pull me through." Fraser was all controlled fury as he explained that it was impossible for him to proceed without it. Holland started to argue again that while he couldn't say what this thing was yet, there was no way he wanted Fraser to have it next to him during the trial.

Judge Turner mulled for a moment, then spoke directly to Fraser. "Mr. Holland was simply saying that he does not consider that thing to be a religious device. He considers it to be a weapon."

Holland nodded.

Turner continued. "I would not, sir, allow that thing to be returned to you so that you could wear it without being satisfied that was a safe thing to do. Quite frankly, I don't like the looks of that thing. And I can't see how anybody would think that would be a religious device."

I could practically hear Holland smile and Harvey sigh.

"So the officer will hold it for you."

Nobody saw that one coming.

"In the public gallery. That way at least it's nearby."

Nobody looked happy about this, especially Harvey. He gently deposited the "power device" on the cushioned bench in the front row of the public gallery. The other officers took this as their cue to leave—fast—and the trial began.

The facts of the case were nasty even by the standards of abuse cases. Fraser hadn't just committed assorted sex acts with his stepdaughters, he'd also chloroformed the girls, tied them up and taken photos. As she sat on the witness stand, Mrs. Fraser explained that, yes, she had known about some of what was going on, but she'd stayed with her husband because she was "a good Christian" and felt it was her duty to preserve their marriage. She'd actually caught Fraser molesting one of their daughters, but after he promised never to do it again, she let it pass. It wasn't until the night she awoke with a headache and found her husband pounding on her skull with a hammer that she finally called the police. That was how he'd earned the attempted murder charge.

I wrote another note to Constable Ron. "Can't you send her to jail too?!"

Fraser stood to cross-examine and looked at his ex-wife

like she was lunch. "I only have one question," he said slowly, purposefully. "Are you still my wife?"

"We got a divorce," she said, sounding certain but ashamed.

"But in the eyes of the Lord, are you still my wife?"

She sat there, trembling, afraid to speak.

After Fraser's ex-wife left, Holland called a psychiatrist as an expert witness. That's when Steve poked his head in the door. He saw Constable Ron next to me and smirked, then turned away from the press box to sit in the public gallery—right next to Harvey and the "meditation device." When Steve moved to touch it, Harvey almost exploded. Figuratively at least.

I tried to wave Steve away, but he just waved back, and the sheriffs scowled like they were going to evict us. The sheriffs weren't going to bother the crazy man with the bomb strapped to his chest, but they were pretty brave about the prospect of tossing a reporter or two out the door. When it became clear the psychiatrist was going to talk in jargon and generalities, I slipped out of the courtroom and into the Crown counsel's office to call Rick. "Hold page one." I'd always wanted to say that. I was sure Rossi said it several times. "You know that figment of my imagination? The bomb squad's flying out from Vancouver to examine it. I'm sure they'll be here any second."

"Bomb squad?"

"Yep."

"Wow." He went quiet for a moment. "But I can't hold page one. The paper will be late."

I couldn't believe this. "All you have to do is give me 12 inches. Dummy in some other story and if I don't get 12 inches in by 5:30, go to press with that."

"I don't know," said Rick. "Stan's not around, so there's nobody here to authorize the overtime."

I was in no mood to argue. "I just spent the entire morning wondering if some lunatic was going to blow up and kill me. As soon as I get home tonight I'm calling this in to the *Province*. So you can either read about it there or the *Trib* can have it first."

Silence at the other end of the phone while Rick figured out whether to hold page one or fire me. Then: "5:30."

Three hours later, just after four, the bomb squad arrived from Vancouver by helicopter. A few local officers joined them outside the courtroom in a police huddle.

"So where's the bomb," asked the squad's leader, a studly looking Marine type with a tough Marine name like Forrest.

"It's in the courtroom," said lovable Glenn O'Donnell.

The four men from the squad started to move en masse. "You can't go in," said O'Donnell.

"What do you mean we can't go in?"

"There's a trial in session."

Forrest looked like O'Donnell had smacked him in the face with a custard pie.

"What the hell are you talking about?"

"Judge's orders," said O'Donnell. "He said the bomb had to stay."

Forrest looked torn between confusion and disgust. "Only in Williams Lake." He'd obviously been here before.

O'Donnell went in to ask the Crown counsel to request a recess. Judge Turner agreed, and the court was cleared. Steve and I stayed—about 30 feet away from the "meditation device"— but we stayed. It only took a few seconds for the squad to make their diagnosis. "It's a homemade pipe bomb. But it's unarmed. All it needs in order to set it off are a couple of shotgun shells."

"The backpack!" I'm not sure who shouted it first, Constable Ron or me.

And while the police went downstairs to find the shells, I ran for the elevator.

Holland stopped me outside the courtroom. "Where the hell are you going?"

"To file my story."

"You can't write about this case. There's a ban."

"There's a ban on talking about the incest trial. You just flew the bomb squad in from Vancouver to dismantle a bomb that was sitting in a courtroom on a judge's orders. That's news."

Holland followed me into the elevator. "You can't print this. I have witnesses coming in tomorrow. His daughters. They'll read it. They'll be afraid to testify."

I heard the words and nodded at him. "I understand," I said.

"Good," he said. "Good."

And I did understand. But I didn't care.

My story was in at 5:45. The bomb story was tough to write because of the publication ban. If I ran Fraser's name I couldn't say he was in court on sexual assault charges. If I ran the charges, I couldn't give Fraser's name. Steve made the decision for me when I heard his radio report while I was typing. He'd gone with the name attached to the tale of the homemade bomb, so that's how I wrote it for the *Trib* and that's how the story would have to read in the *Province*. If I played it the other way I figured I'd be violating the court ban.

I called my editor at the *Province* and explained the situation. He ignored me. "I need the names and charges. That's our policy."

"I can't do that," I said. "There's a court ban."

"They can't stop you from reporting on a man with a bomb. Names and charges."

"It's a sexual assault case, so there's a court ban. The judge will charge me with contempt."

"That's our problem," he said.

"Great," I said. "So if I'm charged with contempt tomorrow, are you gonna fly your best lawyer up to Williams Lake to get me out of jail?"

"Names and charges. That's how we do things in the big city."

"I'll think about it," I said.

"Do that," he said.

I hung up and called the *Sun*.

This time I didn't explain much, but I'm pretty sure I had them at "bomb." I dictated the story to a typesetter before meeting Steve at the Billy. Steve had stayed around long enough to find out that the "device" was actually more complicated than everyone had originally imagined. It was a homemade shotgun, not a bomb. It was capable of firing two shots. And the bullets were in the backpack.

That night Steve and I ordered enough drinks that it was a good thing I lived close enough to stumble home. After each beer we repeated the magic phrase, "If it had been loaded . . . "

Around midnight Steve made a toast. "To life," he said.

And we ordered one last round.

When I got home that night, the phone was ringing. It was the editor of *The Sun*.

"Why haven't you called us about the big sexual assault case?"

"Excuse me?"

"Sixteen counts of sexual assault is big news, Sunshine."

Sunshine? Did I work for this man? At $35 a story, did I need this?

It turned out Steve had reported the sexual assault charges as a separate story. No one would make the connection between that and the bomb story on the radio, but they certainly would in print in a town with two courtrooms.

I tried to explain the situation to the editor, and once again heard all about how it was, "their problem" and I wasn't to worry my small-town head about such things. I told the editor I'd call him back with the story first thing in the morning, as soon as I could check my notes. That was 1986. And I sincerely hope that asshole is still waiting by the phone.

# Play Me a Rock and Roll Song

※

I spent the next day in the courtroom. Fraser was in custody now, but he was still representing himself. His stepdaughters testified. They didn't cry. It would have been easier if they had.

During a break I asked Constable Ron why there were so many cases like this, and he explained that the RCMP had created a sexual abuse team a few months before I'd hit town and as soon as you seriously start looking for dirt, you find it. "It's always been around, but now we're treating it as a crime. Now we know what to look for. And so do the teachers and the doctors and the nurses." I preferred Steve's theory that we were in Canada's Ozarks. That was easier to take than the idea that this really did happen everywhere.

When I turned on the TV that night to watch a cop show, someone pulled a gun—like they normally do on cop shows. I changed the channel. Watching cops and criminals just didn't seem all that entertaining anymore.

The next day Steve and I went for chili at the Friendship Centre. I didn't feel like going into the office. When I walked into work that afternoon, after the trial got out for the day, Abby told me the space shuttle *Challenger* had just exploded.

"How many Williams Lake residents on board?"

Everybody laughed, then said "That's sick." Steve would have been proud.

Just over a week later, I arrived in the office to find out that two trains had crashed near Hinton, Alberta. It was the biggest rail disaster in Canadian history. A VIA Superconductor collided head on with a Canadian National freight train. Twenty-nine people were dead. I'd heard it on the radio on the way to work. This time I didn't make the joke. I should have.

"Two Williams Lake residents on board," said Rick.

I stared at him. He had to be kidding.

"I'm not kidding," he said. "Here's the names. They survived."

I tracked down one of the survivors from the crash. The other survivor was her infant son, and I wasn't sure how to quote a gurgle. Mom was in the third-to-last car of the train, one of the only ones that didn't topple. She was preparing her baby's bottle when the two trains hit. "It felt like it was going over, but it didn't. It was like a miracle."

%

A few nights later I covered "the big concert" of the year. Valdy.

Valdy was a west-coast perennial in the 1980s. When you lived in Vancouver, Valdy was someone you took for granted—a talented folksinger with some lovely tunes and a couple of medium-sized hits, "Peter and Lou" and "Play me a Rock and Roll Song." It seemed like you could see Valdy any time, kind of like Stanley Park. So, naturally, I'd never seen him before. I've been to plenty of big concerts in my life. I saw Fleetwood Mac when they were "the group" of the '70s. I saw David Bowie's "Let's Dance" tour. And I caught Springsteen when he became an American icon with "Born in the USA." And the audience at these concerts couldn't have been any more psyched than the 1,200 people who'd crowded the auditorium at Williams Lake Senior Secondary to hear Valdy.

Everybody was there.

Glenn, Constable Ron and Harvey, people I'd only seen when we were all "on duty," were there in jeans and T-shirts.

There were teachers too—the ones I'd interviewed for my

overcrowding features. And the families from the trailer court. And people I'd seen in the courtroom. And people I'd talked to who I couldn't remember, but who smiled at me just the same as they did when we passed each other in the mall.

Cowboys were there—the folks who'd tried to explain how rodeo events worked. And so were the Indians—Alice from the Friendship Centre and two of the people I'd interviewed who wouldn't go on the record about the slums. I suppose some of the criminals I'd seen in the dockets were there too.

It seemed like half of Williams Lake was at the show—crowded into a high school auditorium, singing along with Valdy and cheering for more. And as I walked to my car that night humming "Peter and Lou," I thought . . . maybe living in a small town's not so bad after all.

# "One Last Trial"

///

In March, the mailroom took a certification vote. People showed up to vote who didn't even work for the paper, people none of us had ever seen. Some mailroom employees turned up and were informed they weren't allowed to vote because they no longer worked at the *Tribune*.

We didn't pay much attention to global news, but the big scandal making headlines at the time was the rigged elections in the Philippines under Ferdinand Marcos. When these strangers started walking in to place their votes, Kate joked, "It looks like a Filipino election." Everyone laughed.

There were a handful of sympathy pickets outside the office that afternoon, guys from local unions who'd shown up in a display of solidarity in the hopes the mailroom staff wouldn't be intimidated.

Steve did a story on the sympathy pickets. The *Trib* threatened to sue the picketers and the radio station. When the vote was counted, the union lost.

I was planning to finally give notice the next day, so I went out with Steve that night to celebrate. I'd just passed buzzed and was halfway to shit-faced when Steve asked about the mailroom vote. I said, "It was like a Filipino election." He laughed. And then he did something that shocked me more than the bomb in the courtroom, more than the Bajardi palaces or the threats to attack me in the parking lot. He took out his notebook.

"What are you doing?"

It was obvious what he was doing. Even drunk out of my skull, I knew what he was doing.

"It's a great quote."

"You can't use it," I said.

"I won't attribute it."

"If they find out who said it, they'll sue."

"I won't tell them who said it. Besides, what do you care? You're leaving."

"They'll think it's Kate." It was Kate. People had heard her.

"So?"

"They'll come after her. Please don't use this. You can't."

"Okay," he said. "Don't worry about it." He shut his notebook and went back to his beer. I couldn't believe he'd even thought of using the quote, and after another cider I'd pretty much forgotten about it. Until the next morning when I was driving to work and turned on the radio.

By the time I got to the office, the company had already threatened a million-dollar defamation suit against whoever made the joke about the Filipino election. Everyone in the newsroom knew it was Kate and assumed she'd told Steve, but no one was ratting her out.

We went for Coney burgers that night, and I told her what happened and begged her to forgive me. She didn't blame me, but if Steve was there I'm pretty sure she would have stuck her fork through his heart.

I waited one more day before walking into Stan's office to give him the news that I was going home. He looked like I'd just handed him a winning lottery ticket. "That's too bad," he said, without even attempting to turn down the wattage of his grin. "But if you really have to go, you should go right away."

"Right a—" I couldn't picture it. I owed him two weeks' notice and that meant I owed two weeks' work.

"We'll pay you for the full two weeks. Don't worry about it."

Worry?

I'd had my final two weeks carefully plotted. There were two trials I was following, and I had to finish my feature on school overcrowding. I'd heard rumours about a doctor who was trading prescription drugs for sex. And I had to do a farewell column.

"Don't worry about it," said Stan. "You can leave at the end of the day."

Rick told me that meant I was done. Somebody else would take my stories.

It felt wrong. And I still wanted to do that farewell column. I had to say goodbye. So I sat at my desk and before anyone decided to escort me out, started to type a summary of the 10 wildest months of my life. I thanked the people I'd interviewed and said goodbye with words that still work for summing up the experience. "It hasn't always been fun, but as I tell everyone constantly—it's never been boring."

I went back to the Women's Centre and, with Kate's help, I packed.

There were about a dozen people at my farewell party the next night. We met at the Billy. The rest of the *Trib* editorial staff was there complete with friends, spouses and dates. It was an odd goodbye. I'd wanted to leave since I got there, but now I felt like a deserter.

Rick quizzed me about my job. He was hoping to take over my beats as soon as the new editor arrived and wanted some tips. As he asked his questions, I thought about how passionately Abby guarded her turf and how I really didn't want to tell Rick any of the secrets I'd fought so hard to learn.

Kevin Holland saw us, pulled up a chair, straddled it and offered to buy me a drink. "You can't go now," he said.

"Why not?"

"There's this case coming up next week that you've gotta cover. The RCMP busted an entire ring of homosexual pedophiles from McLeese Lake. It'll be a great trial."

A gay pedophile rape ring?

Now that's news, Sunshine.

"I guess I could stay and cover it for the *Sun* or the *Province*." All I could think about was how bizarre the story was. My mind had completely blanked out on how little these papers would pay me, if they were still taking my calls.

"And the hockey assault trial is finally making it to court."

Holland grinned. I really wanted to see how that hockey trial turned out.

"Maybe I could do some magazine features on the wild Cariboo." Freelance.

By this time my friends had stopped talking and started staring, wondering if I was going to beg Stan to take me back.

"But I guess there's always going to be one more great story here," I said. "Next week the gay pedophile rape ring, the week after that, another forest fire. There's always going to be something strange happening here."

"It's gonna be a great trial," said Holland.

I'm sure it was.

But the next morning I passed the wooden exit sign on the edge of town for what I was sure would be the last time. And I pulled over on the shoulder to write down what it said: "Thank you for visiting Williams Lake. Goodbye and good luck."

A few months later I was back home, flipping through a magazine in a trendy little bookstore on Robson, Vancouver's trendiest street, when I heard the news on the radio. It was so perfect I phoned the CBC station that afternoon, so I could copy it down word for word.

"The Cariboo region of BC has the dubious distinction of having the highest mortality rate in BC. The health care officer for the area, Dr. John Miller, says he wants to find out why suicides and accidental death rates are much greater than the provincial average. Miller says he's frustrated by the lack of information from Victoria. He says he needs further data to continue his study and to come up with a long-term plan. Suicides are 16 percent above the provincial average, and accidental deaths are 153 percent higher than elsewhere."

I imagined the good doctor driving up to the Cariboo to collect his data, stopping at the Mohawk for gas, telling Tina why he was in town and watching her laugh for a moment before she chirped, "Welcome to Williams Lake."

# Goodbye
# and Good Luck

///

There was a new board game that was popular in the late '80s called "Scruples." It posed hypothetical questions about what you'd do if confronted with certain ethical dilemmas. You and your friends had to predict how you'd respond.

If you'd asked me before I went to Williams Lake what I would have done if someone asked me to interview a grieving widow whose husband died while waiting for open-heart surgery, I would have said I'd quit my job first.

If you'd asked me what I would have done if there was a bomb in a courtroom and I had the chance to run, I'm pretty sure I would have answered "stay"—but only to seem cool. I would have been lying.

And if you'd asked me if I'd be willing to risk my life for a union, for a job I was planning to leave, I would have laughed so hard you wouldn't have had to wait for my answer.

A few months after I left Williams Lake I got a call from Kate to congratulate me. My features on the Bajardis won an honourable mention for the 1986 Canadian Community Newspaper Association's Esso Award for "Outstanding Reporter Initiative" for "a well-written and researched two-part series on housing discrimination against local Native Indians." It was just like Eric had predicted. I was up for an award, and the Bajardis were still charging outrageous rents for places that should have been torched in practice fires.

I didn't have to call Williams Lake to find out Rick Hansen's world tour was over. On May 22, 1987, he returned home after visiting 34 countries and raising over $20 million.

Not long after that I got a call from a friend from my *Ubyssey* days. Scott was a first-year student during my second year at UBC. He said he'd just had the weirdest job interview ever. He'd met the publisher of the *Trib*, and everything seemed to be going well until Stan said, "I see you worked at the *Ubyssey*. Did you know Mark Leiren-Young?"

"Yeah," said Scott."

"And what did you think of him?"

Scott said he could sense it was a trick question, and he didn't want to lose the job. "It felt like he was asking, are you now or have you ever been a member of the Communist party, you know? So I said I didn't know you very well . . . That seemed to be an okay answer. What the hell did you do up there?"

I called Kate to tell her Scott's story. She laughed.

The paper hired two "reporters" to replace me—both with minimal experience but long relationships with Stan. Kate was sure the union wouldn't last long. It made it almost three years.

My union with Barb didn't last anywhere near that long. As soon as I arrived back in Vancouver, our long-distance karma kicked in and she took a job in Prince Rupert.

Kate told me the hockey fight finally made it to trial. Lyle Norton had come up with an even better twist on his defence. He argued that his client was defending the Williams Lake goalie. The case was dismissed. Despite the fact that the accused allegedly jumped on the ice in front of a packed arena, the judge ruled there was "insufficient evidence."

The biggest news story, though, was that Katie Ross was dead. On July 11, 1988, a little less than three years after she'd been acquitted on charges of attempted murder, Katie and her husband were in the woods near Anahim when someone shot at them, killing her husband. Katie made it out and told an RCMP officer that her husband was dead and she'd been shot. The officer didn't believe she was hurt and took her to the nearest medical outpost, where the nurse diagnosed her with "shock."

The nurse suggested that her son drive her to the hospital in Williams Lake, but didn't offer the use of an ambulance, and the Ross family didn't have a pickup. Katie's son finally found a car to borrow and drove his mother to the hospital, where the doctor sedated her. When Katie kept trying to get up to vomit, the hospital staff restrained her on the bed, and that's where they found her the next day.

After she died, 15 hours after she'd told the RCMP officer she'd been shot, someone finally found the bullet hole in her back that had ruptured her abdomen. The death prompted a high-profile coroner's inquest and the creation of a provincial "First Nations Health Liaison Program."

What the stories about the tragedy left out was whether the reason Katie was restrained, the reason she died of sepsis in a hospital bed, was because the staff knew she'd stabbed Mike Tandy and were afraid she was dangerous.

I didn't leave journalism—even though I did produce my play, and it set box-office records for a late-night comedy—but I stuck to freelancing. And the most ironic job I landed came about 10 years after I left the *Trib*, when I was invited to write the introduction to a book on the history of BC community newspapers. I had to do it. I figured it was the perfect way to prove that I hadn't quite been blacklisted.

Almost 20 years later, a friend bought a ranch in the Cariboo, near 100 Mile House. My wife, Darron, and I spent the summer there. I learned to ride. I wore a cowboy hat and cowboy boots. And every time my horse started to gallop, I still heard the "William Tell Overture."

"It's beautiful here," Darron said. "I can't believe you really lived here. Wouldn't this be an amazing place to live?"

After we'd been at the ranch for a week, we drove north to visit Williams Lake.

We arrived just in time for lunch, and pulled into the Dog 'n' Suds to meet Kate, her husband (not Jake) and her daughter—my goddaughter—for Coney burgers and Coney fries. They tasted almost like I remembered them—maybe better because they no longer smelled like tobacco. Even Williams Lake hadn't managed to fight off the smoking ban.

A lot had changed, a lot hadn't.

They still celebrate Wrestling Day. The palaces were still there. Dale Moodie was still missing. And so was D. B. Cooper.

I was right about the Jack of Clubs. It was perfectly safe. It didn't burn down until Valentine's Day, 1994. The Lakeview Hotel, the hotel with no view of the lake, burned down too.

The *Trib* never did find out who made the joke about the Filipino election—and I'm hoping they finally stopped looking. If they didn't, I'm admitting nothing. Steve made it up. Most of the people I worked with are still working at community papers—but not in Williams Lake.

Kate quit the paper to become a union activist. Steve went back to TV news. And Rossi (aka Robert Walden) acted in a reading of my play, *Shylock*, in Los Angeles.

When I was fact-checking for this book, I discovered I still have two sealed envelopes from the ITU that were sent to us just before the vote. I thought about opening them, but decided not to, just in case they have something in them that might convince me I voted the wrong way.

I also called the courthouse to see if I could get access to the transcripts for the biggest trials I'd covered, maybe add some more details. The woman I was shuffled to wanted to know what years they'd taken place. I told her they all happened the same year. She said that didn't seem possible, because she'd heard of all these cases and they were infamous, they were some of the strangest trials in the history of Williams Lake.

I still kind of like country music—especially The Dixie Chicks, CCR, John Fogerty, Kasey Chambers and Johnny Cash.

And, as I write this, that day in November remains the coldest November on record. It was officially -41.6 Celsius the day my car froze, and the all-time record low for Williams Lake is barely one degree lower: -42.8. The old timers were lying about -60.

On the way out of town, Darron and I stopped at the Mohawk to fill the tank. A blonde clerk in her early 40s sold me my Coke. I've kicked the Dubble Bubble habit. I don't think the clerk was Tina, but I didn't ask. I didn't ask how often they'd been robbed recently either.

A few months later I saw a story in the paper declaring that Williams Lake no longer had the highest per-capita crime rate in BC.

I couldn't believe it.

They'd lost the top spot to Smithers. They were number two. I wanted to call Tina to congratulate her, but I had a hunch she'd just tell me they'd be reclaiming the title next year.

# Acknowledgements

I've mentioned a few friends in the introduction, but there's one I didn't write about who deserves most of the credit/blame for bringing this back to life. Tony Wosk read the original manuscript of "City Boy in a Cowboy Town" a few years ago and immediately abused me for abandoning it. Then he told me he only had one problem with it as a book: the original structure was completely chronological, so there was no sense the stories would get as dark as some of them do until almost 100 pages in. Tony wondered why I didn't start with a dramatic incident—"you know, like the bomb in the courtroom, and then you can flash back from there." I'm not sure I slapped my forehead like the guy in those old V8 commercials, but I'm not sure I didn't. I *do* remember that we were in a booth at Hernando's in Toronto, and the moment he said that was the moment I decided to take one last shot at telling these stories.

Thanks to all the people who inspired and encouraged me as a journalist—especially the people who got me to Williams Lake, and the ones who hired me right after I returned from the Cariboo: Nancy Campbell, Charles Campbell, Tom Hawthorn, Maria Hettinger, Dr. Bob Hogg, Peter Ladner, Carol Leiren, Neil Lucente, Verne McDonald, Patrick Murphy, Gordon Murray, Jane O'Hara, Mac Parry, Gary Poole, Glen Sanford, Sid "Who is God" Tafler, Bill Tieleman, Dr. David L. Young and especially my father, Hall Leiren.

Thanks to Vivian Sinclair and Heritage House for believing that you'd want to read this, to Clint Hutzulak for the great design and my editor, Karla Decker, for putting up with me. If you read this and don't spot any glitches, thank Karla. Any "graveyard shit" moments are mine. Thanks to Warren Sheffer for his advice and enthusiasm and to Emma Jordan Leiren Young for being an inspiration.

And a very special thanks to all my friends and colleagues at the *Trib*—and my friends in Williams Lake—whose names I changed and whose stories I turned into composites. You know who you are. I hope you enjoy this, and I hope you know how much I appreciated sharing this ride with you.

Jay Dodge photo

## About the author

Mark Leiren-Young is a screenwriter, playwright, performer and journalist. He wrote, directed and produced the award-winning feature film *The Green Chain*, a documentary-style drama about a dying B.C. logging town.

His stage plays have been produced throughout Canada and the U.S. and have also been seen in Europe and Australia. His scripts *Shylock* and *Articles of Faith* are published by Anvil Press. His satirical comedy troupe, Local Anxiety, has been featured on CBC and NPR and has played major festivals across Canada. Local Anxiety's TV special *Greenpieces* received an EarthVision Award for its satirical take on environmental issues. Mark has released two CDs with Local Anxiety—*Forgive Us We're Canadian* and *Greenpieces*, both of which are available through www.localanxiety.com and iTunes.

As a journalist Mark has written for such publications as *Time*, *Maclean's* and *The Utne Reader*, and he's received a National Magazine Award as a columnist. He's a regular contributor to *The Georgia Straight* and a humour columnist for *The Tyee*, where he also hosts an environmentally themed podcast series, *The Green Chain*, which is available on iTunes. Selected interviews and the screenplay for the movie will be featured in Mark's next book with Heritage House, *The Green Chain: Nothing is Ever Clear Cut*.

Mark currently splits his time between the Sunshine Coast, BC, and Haiku, Maui. For more on Mark, visit his website at www.leiren-young.ca or www.leiren-young.com.